FOUND GODDESSES:

ASPHALTA TO VISCERA

As Revealed to

MORGAN GREY and JULIA PENELOPE

New Victoria Publishers
A Feminist Literary and Cultural Organization

Published by New Victoria Publishers
P.O. Box 27 Norwich, Vermont

Illustrations — Copyright © 1988 by Alison Bechdel
        Cover Illustration and Illustrations on pages i, 2, 18,
        28, 40, 46, 60, 65, 71, 78 88, 94, 100, 110

ISBN 0-934678-18-9
Library of Congress Number 88-062791

Acknowledgements

Any attempt to list the name of every Lesbian or womon who contributed to the Search for Found Goddesses would be ludicrous, and we're going to do it anyway. When we first began our Search for the many Names of They-Who-Watch, innumerable Lesbians and wimmin, revelling in the possibilities and probabilities, quickly set about conjuring both the Names and the Spheres of their lives these Goddesses would affect. We Brainstormed in cars, corridors, and cafeterias, cavorting in creative conjuration. Not all of the Goddesses sought were responsive, so we apologize in advance to friends whose favorite Goddess isn't Invoked in these pages.

Among the friends who re-membered with us are: Debbie Alicen, Kathleen Danker, Sarah Lucia Hoagland, Anne Leighton, Emily Toth, Susan Spencer, The Lincoln Womyn's Spirituality Group, Sally Stoddard, and the womyn of Moon Over Vermont at Goddard College. Jeffner Allen, Joanna Russ, and Elana Dykewomon made useful comments on an early draft of the manuscript.

Readers will recognize the specific, as well as the more general influences of the work of Anne Cameron, Mary Daly (especially *Gyn/Ecology*, *Pure Lust*, and In Cahoots with Jane Caputi, *Websters' First New Intergalactic Wickedary of the English Language*).

Finally, our thanks to Alison Bechdel, whose Wonderful, Lusty drawings grace this book.

Portions of this book have appeared in slightly different form in *SageWoman*, (Vol 1 #1, Fall 1986), *Lesbian Ethics* (Vol. 2 #2, Fall 1986), and *Sinister Wisdom* (#31, Winter 1987).

Notes of Explanation: The first time a goddess is mentioned in a section, Her name appears in caps. Goddesses who also have their own sections are cross-referenced with bold caps.

Authors' Introduction

Once upon a time, not very long ago, a Witch and a Linguist lived in extreme circumstances called Lincoln, Nebraska. As it happened, the Witch (Morgan) knew something of the Craft of Language and the Linguist (Julia) knew something of the Craft of Magic. The underlying principles of language and magic are transformational, and both knew how new realities are created through radical transformations.

One day, we found ourselves in a carload of Dykes circling a parking lot for the umpteenth time (not a magic number!) when one of the Dykes remarked that we really needed a goddess of parking lots. "Yeah!" everyone agreed enthusiastically. No sooner had this chorus subsided than a car pulled out and we were able to park. The conversation ended as the Dykes scrambled out of the car, but the Idea was in the air. A Dyke had voiced her desire; the world was changed.

The Witch and the Linguist knew something momentous when it happened right under our noses. The concept of a modern parking goddess was practical, immediate, and obvious. Why, after all, would Artemis or Demeter wander so far from their ancient spheres of influence to materialize parking spaces? Within days the Goddess of Parking had revealed her name, Asphalta, along with the now-famous parking invocation. Hot on her heels another goddess came trippingly seeking recognition—Pedestria!

Pedestria appeared spontaneously in the midst of the original Blessing of the Shoes ritual. The ritual itself was prompted by the fact that the Linguist had just received a fancy pair of tennis shoes as a gift from a special friend and she wanted to do something to celebrate the neatest shoes she'd ever worn. As it happened, the Witch had bought herself a new pair of shoes just a week earlier, and

1

a shoe blessing ritual sounded like fun. The Lincoln Womyn's Spirituality Group went along with the idea and—Voila!—the Blessing of the Shoes ritual was born. In the midst of our ecstatic reveling, Pedestria revealed herself to us, with the swiftness of Nike and the sheen of patent leather. It was then, with so many goddesses waiting to be found and recognized and named, that the Witch and the Linguist accepted as ours the dis-covering quest that produced this volume.

The Blessing of the Shoes

Finding the modern-day goddesses and skipping through the labyrinthine mysteries that surround each and her proper rituals can be tricky, not to mention risky. We began to realize this several months after the Blessing of the Shoes ritual at which Pedestria had revealed Herself.

Ironically, both the Linguist's and the Witch's new shoes (the only really new shoes at that ritual) began their rapid disintegration, and, within a few months had to be discarded. Apparently, the Blessing of the Shoes ritual needs re-souling. We had goofed somehow, and Pedestria was not pleased. Perhaps the ritual, as recorded here, is too down-at-the-heels, contains something offensive to Pedestria, or omits some element that would insure the longevity of shoes. Clearly, there's nothing patent about the rituals and invocations described here. Should any of you stumble across the proper shoe ritual, please let us know.

Moola-Moola is another goddess who is picky about her rituals. The first Moola-Moola ritual was done by the Witch and her friend Susan. They burned some candles and green incense and made up a dozen or so witty incantations to the great Moola-Moola (only a few of which, fortunately, survived in memory long enough to be written down). The next day, Susan lost her last $10 bill. Needless to say, she thought Moola-Moola had a nasty sense of humor. The next week, however, Susan got a new job with a higher salary.

The Linguist can attest to Moola-Moola's generosity when Her blessing is properly invoked. It was the Witch who cast the spells and aided the Linguist in her first Moola-Moola ritual to sell her house (which had been on the market for two years). The appeal to Moola-Moola was performed on the new moon, and by the following full moon, the Linguist's house had been sold! Moola-Moola, unlike some Found Goddesses, is widely-reputed for Her speed. Within 24 hours of invocations to Moola-Moola (in St. Louis), Julia's friend Sarah won a color television in a grocery store sweepstakes. Since then, the Linguist has twice won money from Lotteria, and Sarah has won a VCR.

This seeching after Found Goddesses began with the Witch's disillusionment about the focus among women's spirituality groups on "lost goddesses." After several years of studying lost goddesses, talking about lost goddesses,

3

teaching classes about lost goddesses, the Witch began to feel that these lost goddesses, while interesting, had no immediate bearing on her life as a Lesbian in the latter part of the Twentieth Century. Those goddesses were defined mostly through their relationships with men and gods, even in feminist writing that tried to re-create older, less male-centered myths, and few of them were Lesbian-identified. Furthermore, not a one of them had ever tried to find a parking space in Manhattan, or wondered, as far as we can determine, what to bring to a potluck.

The Linguist, on the other hand, had not shown one Iota of interest in "lost goddesses," with the possible exception of Eris, the Discordian goddess of chaos. She was into fun and nonsense, being a Dyke in the latter part of the twentieth century, and figuring out how we can use language to create a reality that's comfortable for us.

The Witch and the Linguist got together, and started playing with the idea of creating our own goddesses, FOUND goddesses who not only respond to the specific needs of 20th-century Dykes but whose NAMING calls into being a reality grounded in the will and gynergy of Dyke envisioning. We chortled and guffawed as friends sparked and spun the weird realm of Found Goddesses with us. When we started finding parking spaces with noticeable regularity, and money appeared when we needed it, we knew that our naming and invoking were making a new reality immediate and visible in our lives. Linguists and Witches both, after all, practice the ways language creates and alters the world as we perceive it. What we conceive we name, and the naming makes it so. Our experience with these goddesses has been an empowering one, perhaps because we've had so much fun. Hail, Hilaria!

Since we began our searching for the Found Goddesses, sharing their names and be-ings with other Dykes has brought us much pleasure, for the response is immediate and positive.* Oh, a few have told us loftily that Isis finds their parking spaces, but many have confessed to having

4

their own goddesses for parking and other matters of this world. We've recently learned, for example, that one Dyke's mother, named Laura, always found a place to park as soon as she announced, "Laura's here!," and this invocation to Asphalta continues to work for her daughter and friends. Billie Potts has told us that Dessa is the goddess of Catskills Lesbians, who sign letters "Dessa bless." Another Lesbian told us that a friend of hers, a pantheist, had decided that asphalt, because it is made from things of nature, must still contain some of the spirit of those natural substances. Other womyn, jumping on the concept like ducks on june bugs, have created their own goddesses, one of whom is Serifa, the goddess of typesetters. We suspect that when the typesetting machine breaks down, as it is wont to do, one is Sans Serifa, but this is hard to justify.

The Witch and the Linguist have travelled far and wide in our searches, from the gumbo of Toadstool Park, Nebraska, to the ancient stone circles of New Hampshire, and we've shared many innerviews with the spiritually-inclined, in various attitudes. Nevertheless, this effort is not exhaustive, and many Dykes won't find their particular goddess mentioned here. Goddesses of bowling, broken arms, and hang-gliding haven't yet seen fit to reveal themselves to us, although we know of Dykes who seek them.

Likewise, many goddesses did suggest themselves to us as we carried on, such as Hygeia (the goddess of dental assistants), and Malaria (the humming goddess), but for one reason or another we were unable to dis-cover enough information to include them. On the other hand, we found a Plethora of goddesses concerned with Dyke happiness, perhaps because so many Lesbians want to "be happy," however they define that, or because Lesbians are happier, more satisfied with our lives, than others. Readers may also notice that the names of many of our Found Goddesses begin with "m" or "p," and this we attribute to their labiality.

It is in the spirit of fun and love of Lesbians that we offer you these, our Found Goddesses. Play with them, discover their secrets. If you don't like our goddesses or don't find one that you've been looking for, make up your own. We did. This collection of Found Goddesses is only the beginning, and there is much yet to be dis-covered. Found Goddesses await us in every aspect of our diverse lives!

Not every goddess described here will be of equal importance to each Dyke's experience, but we think there's at least one goddess recorded in these pages who'll show Herself to be useful in some Dyke's struggle to survive well. For example, Asphalta is important if you drive a car, but Transportia better addresses the needs of Dykes who ride busses a lot. If you're opposed to chemicals of any sort, but particularly those that are addictive and destructive, only some aspects of Chemia will be relevant to your life, and you'll find Detoxia more appropriate to your concerns. If you're an incest survivor who mistrusts touching, Cuddles may not be a goddess you'll cherish, but if, like Ruth Mountaingrove,** you're exploring "the ethics of nourishment," then Cuddles may speak eloquently to your experience.

However you respond to these goddesses, finding and naming those that reflect your experience is an **active** exploration. We can't sit around and **wait** for our goddesses to find us! We need the creative imaginings of all Dykes in our lives. Transforming reality through visioning is the essence of Wiccacraft. Share your dis-coveries and researches with us. We'd love to hear what you find. So mote it be!

---

*Several years after we had started this book, we were delighted and once again made aware of synchronicity in our lives by Gail Saussier's mention of "Tofushu," Lesbian goddess of potlucks, in *Lesbian Etiquette*, Freedom, CA: Crossing Press, 1985.

**Ruth Mountaingrove, "Touch: The Ethics of Nourishment" in *Lesbian Ethics* Vol. 1, #3 [1985:26-29].

AEREA CORRIDA, She-Who-Flies-the-Friendly-Skies, is often worshipped, like **ASPHALTA**, as one of the goddesses who protects the delicate processes of establishing and maintaining Lesbian Connections. Every village, town, and city has at least one major temple where offerings can be made to this goddess. Large cities may have neighborhood temples as well, called Branches. Within these Branches, devotees line up before small windows where they make offerings to the priestesses, who reward Aerea Corrida's faithful with small gummy squares which they joyfully lick with their tongues.

Her major temples, often known as the Downtown Branch, are haphazardly located in large cities, in areas that challenge even Asphalta's propensity for parking places, and appeals to Her have been known to fail in the vicinity surrounding one of Aerea Corrida's temples because She is so popular. Therefore, many devotees prefer to invoke the services of **PEDESTRIA**, observing that Aerea Corrida has so many small shrines everywhere that appeals to Asphalta are needless when one has merely to walk down to the corner of almost any street to make an offering of cards or letters. Indeed, it is true that Aerea Corrida has shrines conveniently located, and those who seek Her need only look for a bright blue metal container with a rounded top.

A caution is necessary at this point, however. Nothing is as simple as it seems. Some initiates into the mysteries of

7

Aerea Corrida report the existence of shrines to a false goddess who de-lights in leading the followers of Aerea Corrida into error. These false shrines have the same shape so beloved of Aerea Corrida, but they're an unmistakable bile green. Ritual gifts offered to Aerea Corrida at these fake shrines never reach their destination, and many Lesbian Connections have been broken as a result of this error. Such offerings are said to be lost among the males, where they become Dead Letters; they are but are not. In the event that you have unknowingly committed such an error, it's always a good idea to invoke **EVACUA** as soon as you realize it with a quick incantation, like "Oh Shit!" Whatever you deposited in the false shrine still won't get where you wanted it to go, but your conscience will be clear.

It is widely held that Aerea Corrida, in Her FLIGHTY aspect, is the special guardian of those Lesbians called, variously, Flakes or Airheads, who are renowned for their love of communing ecstatically and frequently in ethereal realms. These devotees of Aerea Corrida, also called Space Cadets, are inclined to Flights of Fancy, during which they babble incantations said to be in the ancient Mother Tongue. Friends claim that Space Cadets do not "Have Their Feet on the Ground," because the surest way to get their attention is to chant "Earth to _____" several times in succession, supplying the name of the spaced-out friend. Should this chant fail to retrieve the Space Cadet from Outer Space, her friends may withdraw, mumbling "She's in a weird space today."

Some Lesbians, believing that the path to Be-ing requires "Having One's Feet on the Ground," allege that Space Cadets indulge too frequently in the rituals sacred to certain aspects of CHEMIA, like MARIJUANA or EL ES DIA. Others say that Flakes, Airheads, and Space Cadets are among those especially favored by Aerea Corrida in spite of the fact that their observance of Her rituals is erratic and unreliable.

Finally, there are some Lesbians said to shun the worship of Aerea Corrida altogether, whether out of laziness or principle isn't altogether clear. Sometimes regarded as irreverent by devoted observers of Her rituals, these Nag-Gnostics* are said, nevertheless, to have redeeming qualities, and atone for their lack of Correspondence by surprising their friends with spontaneous rituals under the auspices of SPRINTA or MA BELL. These attentions are irregular, unpredictable, and of infrequent occurrence, and have been known to happen at inconvenient times. Nag-Gnostics counter this by pointing out that Aerea Corrida isn't so dependable either, and the issue of Corresponding and the proper Maintenance of Connections remains up in the air.

---

*For the origin and meaning of *Nag-Gnostic*, see: Mary Daly, *Pure Lust*, (Boston: Beacon Press, 1984), p. 12, and, In Cahoots with Jane Caputi, *Websters' First New Intergalactic Wickedary of the English Language*, (Boston: Beacon Press, 1987), p. 147, hereafter cited as *The Wickedary*.

ANIMA gives us paws in the busy-ness of our daily lives, renewing our spirits so that we may rise above the litter scattered within our minds. It is She who watches over the connections Lesbians share with animals of all types, both those who live with Lesbian companions and those who live apart. The devout are said to eat only the small cookies blessed by Anima's priestesses, called Anima Crackers. So rigorous is this regimen that some have been known to go Crackers, entering into a state of permanent bliss.

Lesbians, especially Healers, have long been known for their connections with animals. While traditional wisdom links Lesbians with cats, for many of us live with one or several cat companions, it is also true that many Lesbians form strong ties with animals of all species: dogs, goats, rabbits, birds, fish, snakes, lizards, spiders, gerbils, and turtles, but especially those that share with us the Lesbian reproductive process known as Parthenogenesis. So widespread is the worship of Anima that covens devoted to Her worship, sometimes called "teams," bear the names of Her beloved companions: the Wildcats, Cubs, Tigers, Lions, Dolphins, Redbirds, etc. Those touched by the love of Anima are recognized by their animal spirits, and often experience a trance called Animation, during which they come within a whisker of melting into Her Be-ing.

Anima is known by many names in many aspects. As FELINA she teaches us the ways of true luxury, the abandon of playfulness and the pleasures of our senses, and in this aspect may be familiarly addressed as "Kitty, Kitty." It's not unusual late at night to hear devotees of Felina walking the streets calling out, "Here Kitty, Kitty," for She loves the cover of night and the darkness, often retiring to Catacombs for Her naps. She is particularly fond of shag rugs and soft pillows, especially in the sunlight, and Her followers often make pilgrimages to Catalina in order to catch the rays. These devout are sometimes called "Crispy Critters" when they indulge too much in such observances. One of Her most popular rituals is called The Catnap. Awakened abruptly from one of these rituals, She has been known to go into Catniption Fits, hurling hairballs in every direction. Those struck by these missiles are said to be "Hair Today, Goon Tomorrow."

From Her we learn to remain watchful in rest, and to move quickly from deep sleep to full alertness in danger. Her priestesses, widely known for their inscrutable wisdom, are often said to be "Catty," a psychic state induced by one of the herbs sacred to **CHEMIA,** known to initiates as Catnip. These adepts, who, it is said, have grasped the mysteries of Cataclysms and Catalytic Converters, weary of the world and retire to temples of meditation called Cathouses.

Her most favored devotees can be recognized by the dusty paw prints that adorn their cars, and the many tiny scars they bear proudly on their hands and arms, which, they say, are earned in observances called Cat Fights, which, because of their Animosity, are shunned by the mousey. In Her ferocious appearances, Felina is shown with arched back and raised tail, a stance often adopted by her worshippers during Cat/astrophes.* Objects sacred to this aspect of Anima include catamarrans and catalysts, and Her

11

rituals are said to be most successful if observed in a grove of catalpas. Incantations to Felina—Catcalls—are used to invoke Her for tranquility or rage, depending on the need of the devotee.

To call upon Felina in a meditative mood, the following incantation is said to be purrfect:

Felina, Felina, don't be a tease,
Come lull me, lull me, my purrpose is peace.

Felina, wise fur purrson, please get to it:
Teach me your calm, I know you can do it.

Some thearists have suggested that a ritual now sacred to **UMPIRA** was originally linked to the worship of Felina because of her love of playfully batting balls about, but the doubtful insist that more fieldwork must be done before such a connection can be asserted.

Followers of other aspects of Anima, such as the toothsome CANINA, enjoy subjects and objects they can "sink their teeth into" and "chew on," and are known for their love of ideas and lengthy analysis. It is said they are dogged in this pursuit, and one of their rituals begins when a participant says, "I have a Bone to pick." Offerings to Canina, called Scraps, or Dogma, are carried about in paper containers, known to the devout as Doggie Bags. One adept priestess has invented a machine for processing these Scraps, the Dogmatic, which is started by pushing buttons. Once the offerings to Canina have been prepared dogmatically, they are woofed down.

It has been suggested that Canina, in fact, may have been a friend or lover of **VISCERA**,an intimacy still celebrated in observances during which emotions are unleashed and run wild, called Puppy Love. The celebrants are mysteriously drawn to one another, and much Heavy Petting is said to go on. Rituals to Canina are most successful when performed during that season sacred to Her, the Dog Days, or within a grove of Her beloved Dogwood trees. Few stray.

Virtually every city or town has at least one temple to Anima, called the "Humane Society" (why, we don't know) or the "Anima Shelter," where the creatures sacred to Her are given care until they pick out a Lesbian companion suitable to them. Should you wish to become a companion to Anima's chosen, particularly those called the Paws that Refresh, you must visit one of these temples frequently, no matter how fur you have to go, making the appropriate cooing and cuddling noises that attract Her favor. Eventually, one (or more!) of Her creatures will choose you and come to live with you, for a small cash offering. The Sign of your Choosing will be a Lick and a Promise, Blessed Anima!

---

*An event precipitated by Catty Conspirators that subverts the patriarchal order or system of things" (from *The Wickedary*, p. 111).

ANOMIA's influences are felt in the lives of all Lesbians, for silences surround us. Anomia guards the secretive and the hidden, and discreetly camouflages the entrances and exits of Closet Lesbians, who do not wish to be Visible. For this reason, one of Her aspects, MARGINALIA, is believed to have in-spired the works of Anonymous, one of our most prolific writers.

Those who seek Anomia's cloistered benevolence are often heard to invoke Her by intoning words like "discretion" and "respectability," and they are much given to chanting phrases of dubious meaning, such as "What I do in bed is no one's business" and they are given to many silences about themselves. Many devotees of Anomia are also known as Yuppies to their detractors, and avoid Lesbians they regard as "indiscreet," "blatant," or "obvious." The priestesses of Anomia are in the habit of wearing vestments called Polyester Pantsuits, or Designer Labels. They shun other labels that they claim are too "limiting."

Anomia's sacred lawns and tulip gardens can be found only in Sub-Urbia, where Her clandestine mysteries are celebrated. A ritual begins when one of Her priestesses asks, "What's in a Name?," and the gathered worshippers turn to one another and introduce themselves as Mary, Sue, or Jane, carefully omitting second names. Everyone then chants "The Name Game," one of Anomia's most popular hymns, in unison, for its tongue-twisting reversals

14

celebrate the ancient Lesbian rite of taking a Pseudo-name. In the "old days," it is said, many Lesbians, fearful of exposure and ruin, adopted Pseudo-Names when they joined the Daughters of Bilitis. This ritual honors those who have gone before.

Anomia can be invoked by calling out cheerily, "Got the Name, Play the Game," but only in the State of Privacy. Those blessed by Anomia may dwell in the relative safety of Sub-Urbia, provided they shun the Mailing Lists cherished by COLLATEA's (see **LABOREA**) followers, return (unopened) any Third Class mail sent to them by groups having the L-word in their names, and inscribing such stray missives with the sacred words, "No Such Person, No Such Address." "Moved, Left No Forwarding Address" will, they say, work quite as well.

Devotees of Anomia are known to frequent the observances sacred to **PARANOIA**, where they sometimes inadvertently Rub Shoulders with political activists, whom they call "Extremists." The two groups do not mix well. One indisputable authority has traced the Act of Heavy Stapling, an indulgence of the Ambitious Amazons, to followers of Anomia, who also cherish items brought to them under **AEREA CORRIDA**'s auspices in Plain Brown Wrappers.

Her shrines, called "closets," are to be found in the houses and apartments where many Lesbians live, and it is a sign of affluence to have more than one in which to hide one's secret offerings to Anomia. Similarly, the size and spaciousness of one's closet symbolize one's devotion to Anomia, and "walk-in closets" are much prized among the faithful.

Anomia, who dwells in the Places Where Words Are Not,

can also be invoked as She Who Guards Our Silences, both chosen and unchosen, for who can say what Lesbians choose or do not choose? This is one of Anomia's Great Mysteries, and a source of much thealogical debate. Reformist Anomians insist that failure to observe Her Secretive Silences involves great risks, while Radical Anomians (also called Pronomians) are committed to saying the L-word out loud, often in Public Places, a practice they call Breaking Silence.* Some Anomians, unable to decide which observance is the most effective, practice both rituals of Silence, just in case. Sacred to Her are the varied Phases we go through, for one may be In as well as Out of Phase. She is to be found in all the spaces of our lives and experiences for which the language of the fathers fails us, but especially Her Presence fills those moments of intense, indescribable feelings among Lesbians, those times when we weary our tongues seeking the word, the articulate form to say what is for us. She is also, then, invoked when we wish to break our silences and offer the Gift of Meaning to an Other.

Some Lesbians, inspired or frightened by their intense feelings for each other, perhaps under the spell of **EUPHORIA** or **VISCERA**, are said to be blessed by VERBENA when words pour from their mouths with a richness and quantity like unto our menstrual flows. Unfortunately, these outpourings sometimes fail to "make sense" to others but we regard them as the beautiful offerings that they are. Such observances are known, among the devout, as Tongue-in-Cheek.

We have found no goddess willing to look favorably upon lies, deceptions, or purposeful omissions (which are properly regarded as the work of **QUIETUS**), but an aspect of Anomia, calling Herself Marginalia, has as Her Sphere our

16

perpetual proclivity for Self-Erasure. She has revealed Herself as in-spiring the numberless works of Anonymous, our Foresister, and of all those whose good works have been lost and forgotten. It is said that this aspect of Anomia is often the cause of our forgetfulness of our herstory, our tendency to distort and exaggerate events and reactions, and responsible for our unintentional omissions, because we have internalized the belief that our lives and deeds are insignificant. In Marginalia, we confront the fears we haven't named to ourselves, whereby we confound ourselves. Marginalia, one of Anomia's oppressive aspects, is present to us in the midst of our silences of dis-ease, of anger for which words are insufficient, of dis-comfort and tension, or when we unhappily find ourselves ms.-speaking.

Ritual observances to this goddess are always being Phased In or Phased Out, depending on the Political Climate. Yet, our recognition of Anomia in all of Her aspects enables us to unravel the bindings forged by patriarchal language to develop our own ways of speaking among ourselves. For this reason, Anomia is often known to reveal Herself to us in those moments when we take Great Risk.

---

*For the patriarchal meaning of the phrase "Breaking Silence" and how it has stifled Lesbian nuns, see *Lesbian Nuns: Breaking Silence*, edited by Rosemary Curb and Nancy Manahan (Tallahassee: Naiad Press, 1985).

A priestess of Asphalta

ASPHALTA, goddess of all roads, streets, and highways, and guardian of those who travel on them, is best known for Her miraculous powers of finding parking places. The formal Parking Place Invocation to Asphalta, chanted by Her devotees around the world, and never known to fail when sincerely uttered, even in impossible-to-park-in cities like New York and Montreal, is:

Hail, Asphalta, full of grace:
Help me find a parking place.

This invocation should be intoned at least two blocks before you want to park, although it has been known to work on very short notice. A brief version of the invocation, developed by followers of Asphalta in Chicago, "Asphalta, do Your Thing," has also proven to be effective. In the event that Asphalta has created an ideal parking place, and some rude motorist attempts to take it away, chant:

Hail, Asphalta, full of grace:
Keep that pud out of my space.

Asphalta is one of the most widely-worshipped of all modern Found Goddesses. Her highways and streets form complex intersecting webs which join Her many thousands of temples and shrines, and connect the lives of Lesbians. Her major temples are located wherever road construction is underway, and are attended by Her High Priestesses, who usually wear jeans or overalls, boots, hardhats, and colorful scarves or handkerchiefs about their necks or heads, as well as vestments of Her sacred color, day-glo orange. They often carry flags or signs as symbols of their high office. All motorists slow down when passing through one of Asphalta's Sacred Places, and stop when instructed to do so by a priestess, who should always be addressed as "Most Esteemed Flagwomon." Failure to heed the signals of a priestess has been known to have fatal consequences, but those especially cherished by Asphalta may be given the Sacred Baton to pass to a traveler going in the opposite direction. The ritual of Passing the Sacred Baton symbolizes the continuity as well as the diversity of our paths.

Asphalta's shrines, marked by heaps of concrete and asphalt left after a temple has moved, are usually unattended and visited only by Her most devoted followers, who sometimes carry a relic from one of these places (a small crystal of asphalt, in a bright orange bag with a yellow cord) around their necks or hanging from the rearview mirror of their car. These relics are said to have great powers, and will guarantee safe passage from one place to another. Especially renowned for their shifting powers and much sought after by frequent travelers, are the rare Asphalt crystals that have part of the Yellow Line in their matrix. The Yellow Line is widely held to represent the Order of Society and Social Contracts. For this reason, many thearists suspect that Asphalta is actually a major goddess whose influence extends far beyond roads and travel. Indeed, Her intersecting webs connect all that Is.

INTERSTATIA is one of Asphalta's best-known aspects, although each town and city has its own names for this deity. She sometimes appears as Toll Road or Tollway, and is reputed to be both convenient and expensive, for, at varying distances from each other, one will find small shrines to Asphalta. It is said that making an offering to a priestess at one of these shrines, called Toll Booths, insures the traveler's safe passage from one shrine to the next. Some devotees, anxious to travel as quickly as possible from one point to another, are known to buy Monthly Books of Coupons, which they use as offerings. Interstatia's symbol is the Cloverleaf, and many report exceptional effects when **MOOLA-MOOLA**'s favorite color, green, is combined with the Cloverleaf and worn as an amulet.

CHANCY, our goddess of unpredictable edibles, protects our weighs and means, and hears our woes and moans. She is particularly popular in Lesbian communities, where she is worshipped in ritual feasts known as "potlucks." Like the Chinook ceremonial feasts, called *potlatch* (from Nootka *patshatl*, giving or gift), from which our potlucks are descended, we celebrate our free giving to one another. Each member of the community brings with her some favorite dish of food as an offering, and these offerings are then displayed together on however many tables are required for their appreciation. Before the revelers are permitted to break these foods together, they must circle each table at least once, uttering "oohs" and "aahs" before each offering, and ask "What is that?" and "Who brought it?"

The substance of the ritual begins when one reveler turns to another and asks, "What do you think is in it?" and the response is, "Chancy." After Chancy has been invoked by these questions and appropriate noises, the hungriest participants race for the plates to see who can fill hers to overflowing the fastest. This is said to be "helping oneself" and it must be accomplished with great relish. It is often said, "To the quick, variety." Casual worshippers, slow to help themselves to Chancy's bounty, often find they must make a meal of clam dip and dried oatmeal cookies.

If, by Chancy, the plates available on that day are made of flimsy paper, overfilling can result in overspilling, where-

21

upon more appropriate noises are forthcoming from the revelers. If the potluck occurs outdoors, under a full moon, the quantity of food dropped to the earth is taken as a measure of Chancy's favor. Those who leave nothing to Chancy are at great risk. Each tribe, of course, has its own way of worshipping Chancy, but it is She who watches over the selection and preparation of recipes. She is, therefore, one of our goddesses of inspiration, and her devotees have been known to concoct veritable, edible delights from leftovers, which are sacred to Chancy. Woe unto her who, uninspired or neglectful, makes an offering of Kentucky Fried Chicken, with only eleven herbs and spices. She will quickly find herself over a barrel, and her cries of "Finger-lickin' good" will avail her naught. "'Tis better," it is said, "to take one's chances with tofu and soy sauce."

Chancy is well-known for her peculiar and unpredictable sense of humor and her utter disregard for the principles of nutrition and aesthetics. She delights and exults in feasts consisting only of desserts or breads, and her worshippers fondly recall their salad days and entire meals of just desserts. These, however, have become rarer as the years pass.

CHEMIA, goddess of the "change through pleasure" principle, appears to Her devotees in many forms, for pleasure has many faces. As Chemia, Her Essence can be invoked by calling upon MARIJUANA, SENSEMILLA, PSILOCYBA, EL ES DEA, COCA-COLA, and INTOXIA. Her adherents are known to ingest various chemical substances as a result of which they report heightened pleasure or relaxation, but most celebrate altered states of consciousness during which they say Chemia visits them with inspiration and the insight to change their lives. Truly, it is said, "Without Chemia, life would be impossible." Worshippers of ACHEMIA (see **DETOXIA**) claim that this slogan is inaccurate and misleading, but, then, who's to say what the real thing is? Debates over "the REAL thing" have raged in Lesbian communities recently, dividing Chemia's worshippers, who can't seem to agree on what "it" is. Some have switched to the "New Coke," calling Nutrasweet a new treat from Chemia, but devotees of "Classic Coke" claim that Nutrasweet is a false, politically incorrect goddess. A small portion of Chemia's worshippers, in a fit of nostalgia, have pledged themselves to "Cherry Coke" who, they say, will make their lives more fruitful.

In Her more mundane aspects, Chemia enters our homes and our lives as LYSOLA, OXYDOLY, BONA AMIA, and PALM OLIVIA, through them bestowing upon us the assorted, and unsung, blessings of Dyke Domesticity (see also **LABOREA**). The followers of Chemia in Her mundane aspects are well-acquainted with the experience of

23

infinity, which Meryl Natchez* says is revealed in the tasks of washing dirty dishes and cleaning house. For those inspired by the blessings of SANIFLUSH or EASY OFF, "cleanliness is next to Nothing."

In some communities, the mundane aspects of Chemia are celebrated at the Vernal Equinox with an annual Dyke Domesticity Contest. Those devotees compulsive enough to try, engage in a year-long festival of house-cleaning, scrubbing their woodwork, ironing their sheets, and flushing their toilets. These rituals must be performed in a frenzy. Their joy, they say, has many folds, and Chemia puts a shine in their lives. They suffer not from the demons Static Cling or Ring-Around-the-Collar. DD points are awarded haphazardly to those who draw attention to their spiritual work, and, at the end of a year, someone declares herself the Domestic Dyke of the Year. If her claim is challenged, the entire community is called upon to sniff, finger, and open drawers to determine the truth of the conflicting claims. Consensus rarely occurs.

The followers of the mundane Chemia in all Her aspects are much-beloved and sought-after in collectives and political action groups because of their obsession with doing everything "just so." It is said, and truly, that any group blessed with one of these cannot fail, for they love the clean sweep with a new broom. Others, envious perhaps, have been heard to mutter, "Nature abhors a vacuum."

Some do not do windows.

------

*Paraphrased from a calendar page our friend Susan saved and hung on her kitchen wall. We do not know who Meryl Natchez is, or what calendar it was. Much is lost to us, but we honor a name saved from the masses of Anomia.

24

CHOCOLATA is believed by many to be merely an occasional, or periodic, aspect of **MUNCHIES**, because She frequently appears only at specific times during a lunar cycle or under similar conditions. Her most devoted adherents, however, who are legion, maintain that Chocolata is a major goddess, deserving ritual observances of Her own. Devotees of **TOFU, MISO, and SOYA** are known to invoke the deity CAROB, claiming that the delights of Carob are indistinguishable from those of Chocolata and, besides, "better for you." These are major thealogical debates unlikely to be settled in the near future, and we won't try to resolve them here. Of more importance, we believe, are indications that some forms of Chocolata worship can be traced back to the Amazons.

What we have been able to find out suggests diverse connections between the rituals of Chocolata and the most ancient roots of our own spirituality. Chocolata is often found in small, edible statues that resemble bunnies or cream-filled eggs (around the time of the Vernal Equinox), or fat, bearded figures with bags slung over their shoulders around Winter Solstice, and in small pointed breast-like pieces commonly called "Kisses." One researcher on goddess worship has suggested that both the shape and the name of these "Kisses" point to an intimate relationship between the rituals of Chocolata, during which loud sucking sounds are made, and those of **CUDDLES, LILI-HA'ALA'A**, and LABIA (both Minora and Majora). One linguist, who has spent much of Her life decoding the ancient language of the Amazons, has discovered that the mysterious name, M & Ms, is an esoteric aspect of Chocolata that means "Menstruation and Menopause."

Further evidence can be found in the custom of exchanging heart-shaped boxes of Chocolata tokens (the heart being a well-known symbol of Liliháaláa in the Old Religion), while chanting the invocation, "Be my Valentina." The origins of such customs, while obscure, have much in common with the rituals of Liliháaláa, **NEMEHA'ALISH**, and Cuddles, which are generally regarded as pleasurable and, therefore, much sought after. Devotees of all three goddesses have been known to smile broadly after a ritual enactment, and report a sense of well-being and contentment. Much licking of the fingers is also a common ritual activity. Given the increasingly strong evidence of long-standing associations between Chocolata, **EUPHORIA**, Cuddles, Nemeháalish, and Liliháaláa, we find it difficult to dismiss Chocolata's significance out of hand.

Worshippers of Chocolata are sometimes secretive about their rituals, but certain tell-tale signs signify that ritual indulgence has occurred. The most common include small, brown smudges around the lips and chin, sticky fingers, and a serenity of spirit verging on Euphoria's blessing. Lesbians who speak of "melting in one's hands" or "a month of sundaes" may well be fudging.

Of special importance, we think, are the reports of many Lesbians who feel an increased longing and enthusiasm for the rituals of Chocolata, Cuddles, and Liliháaláa one week before the onset of menstruation. Surely this cannot be a casual relationship.

CUDDLES, too, is one of the popular and much-worshipped goddesses of bodily pleasures. Her rituals are observed frequently and repeatedly for the warmth and sense of well-being She in-spires in Her devotees. These call themselves Friends, which means 'Free One' (*frēond*, after the manner of the Amazons of Albion in the Golden Age).* She is an easy goddess, always accessible and accommodating, and Her presence can be invoked by the gentlest caress or the tightest hug. Wherever Lesbians greet one another with hugs, kisses, and laughter, there, also, is Cuddles, dancing among the encircled arms, savoring the heat that rises as hands touch and lips meet. Cuddles is especially fond of the feelings aroused when breasts are pressed against breasts and nipples rise in taut greeting.

Some particular friends have developed these rituals into a fine art form. They've practiced a lot, but gladly admit that even they are still perfecting the sensuality of their observances. Frequency of worship apparently heightens the pleasure of Cuddles' indulgences. It has been said that one can easily identify a Lesbian among all others by observing how she performs Cuddles' rituals, for Lesbians don't hold back any part of their bodies when they invoke Her, eagerly sharing full body contact when they hug.

Cuddles, however, like so many other goddesses, is unpredictable, and revels in the energy sparked during even the briefest hugs!

*References to the Amazons of Albion and the Golden Age are from Monique Wittig and Sande Zeig, *Lesbian Peoples: Material for a Dictionary*, NY: Avon, 1976. For more information about the Old English meaning of *frēond* see *Webster's Seventh New Collegiate Dictionary* (1972), p. 335; also "Intertextuality: The Language of Lesbian Relationships" by Debbie Alicen, *Trivia* 3, Fall 1983, p. 6+.

OBSERVING THE RITES OF CUDDLES: MOTION STUDY

FRAME 1: THE SIGHTING

FRAME 2: THE APPROACH

FRAME 3: FULL CONTACT

DEA ABLEA, the goddess of fitness chic, is widely worshipped for Her muscled physique and fabled strength. The arduous rituals of Her followers are observed with fervor and determination, believed by some to verge on the fanatical, often to the exclusion of all other bodily pleasures. Even among Her devotees it is acknowledged that Her strenuous rituals can be addictive. Some, perhaps erroneously, confuse Dea Ablea with **EXERTIA**, but we cannot be certain of this.

Her temples, called Spas or Gymnasia, are currently enjoying a surge of popularity, and small, underequipped shrines to Dea Ablea called "weight rooms," can be found in YWCAs. Some of these temples are open 24 hours a day for the observances of Her muscled devotees, but the offerings demanded are said to be Out of Line by the skeptical.

Seeking the ecstasy of pushing their stamina beyond its limits, devotees of Dea Ablea may begin a ritual by jogging ten miles (as quickly as possible), followed by 50 or 200 sit-ups, and five miles in a swimming pool (Dea Ablea isn't picky about the stroke as long as it is swift and smooth).

The more difficult and prolonged the exertions of Her rituals, the longer Her devotees can stay afterward in a sauna or hot tub. In addition to their daily devotions, which must be observed regularly to earn the favor of Dea Ablea, Her high priestesses also participate in extravagant Marathon ritual observances on the Days sacred to Dea Ablea, often traveling far from their homes, and at great personal expense, to seek Her Blessings. It is said that Dea Ablea is particularly pleased by gradual increases in speed, distance, strength, and endurance among Her worshippers, and Runners of the Marathon are known to be among Her most cherished.

Skeptics who have the temerity to scoff at the sacred rituals for Dea Ablea and the sincerity of Her devotees, say that the followers of Dea Ablea are more taken with sweat and the colorful sweatsuits they wear, which are often accompanied by matching sweatbands and tennis shoes as accessories. Although they will deny it if confronted, Her followers have been known to worship lesser goddesses, such as NIKE, PUMA, and JANTZEN, if they believe they can get away with it, and some have been discovered seeking the benevolence of **TOFU, MISO, and SOYA, DE-TOXIA**, or, alas, **PEDESTRIA**. They claim that, far from being digressions from the Path of Bodily Perfection, these observances enhance their devotion to Dea Ablea. They hint that THERE ARE MANY WAYS.

Dykes who are not particularly fervid can still maintain the façade of fitness chic, without the aroma, by wearing the coordinated sportswear so adored by Dea Ablea, but only if they have no apparent disabilities and aren't fat. A fat Dyke, thinking perhaps to pass as a devotee of Dea Ablea by donning Her ritual garb, will likely find Herself mocked and ridiculed for Her presumption. Disabled Dykes, always ready of wit, rightly observe that the most devoted of Dea Ablea's worshippers are prone to disabilities of many kinds, the pains of which accompany them even into their Cronehood. These they call TABS, the Temporarily Able-Bodied. In wit, there is wisdom.

DETOXIA, a goddess to whom transition and struggle are dear, is said to be one of the most difficult of the Found Goddesses in Her observances, and Her Paths frequently prove to be tricky and full of potholes for those who would undertake Her rituals of abstention and self-purification. Those who forego the pleasures of **CHEMIA** seek, thereby, to rid their bodies of patriarchal poisons and to clear their minds of the Fathers' Fog.

Her devotees shun the liquid gifts of INTOXIA, which they regard as deceptive and illusory. Many Lesbians who once sought the false comfort of Intoxia's libations, awake one day with the DTs (Dyke Traumas), and know they have not chosen wisely. In an A-mazing Act of Strength, they vow to shun the temptations of Intoxia and undertake spiritual quests known as "Going on the Wagon" or "Going Cold Turkey." These are arduous journeys. Through their observances of Detoxia's cleansing rituals, many Dykes learn to forsake their destructive dependence on Chemia, and it is the spirit of Detoxia that guides them along the path from Chemia to the sweet breath of ACHEMIA, our goddess of chem-free space.

Like **DEA ABLEA**, Detoxia requires constant attention to Her observances and rituals, and those who would follow Her Path must show constant vigilance and an unswerving will to change. To those who have the desire, Detoxia smiles, but She is never gentle.

DIGITALIS, called Lady Fingers by Her intimates, is both dexterous and sinister. She is Our-Goddess-of-Computers, for She protects those who attend to the Mysteries of Software and Hardware, those who Program and those who Reprogram. Devotees of Digitalis can often be found gazing enchantedly into a small screen, tapping happily upon their beloved Keyboards. Many are known to experience trances when the Presence of Digitalis "carries them away." Indeed, those Lesbians who worship Her at home say that their computers are Personal.

Her sacred observances include Digital Manipulation, Counting to Ten, and Going with the Program. She is sometimes invoked for the purpose of Calculation, the adding up and subtracting of Digits, and for this reason Her rituals are at times associated with those of **FALLOPIA**.

Digitalis can be invoked by humming the tune, "Finger Poppin' Time," or by intoning Her well-known incantation, "Let Your Fingers Do the Walking." Among Her sacred relics are Digital Clocks and Watches, Touch-tone Phones, and She is inordinately fond of those who observe Her by Staying in Touch. Her sacred stone is the Quartz Crystal, for its properties of conveying the electrical charges known to pass among Her devotees. Initiates into Her many mysteries are adept at Putting their Fingers on a variety of things, and they often acknowledge their allegiance to Digitalis by keeping Her rites in dark shrines which they call Pockets. These Pockets are both small and large, and it is rumored that bands of Her devotees gather in Pockets of Unrest or Disturbance, but we have been unable to confirm the existence of such covens.

An important aspect of Digitalis, known to Her followers as THE GLITCH, deserves more attention in Dyke circles than She currently enjoys. It is the special function of The Glitch to foul up the computer networks created by men, the megacomputers that compute and transmit such things as telephone, heating, and electric bills to Dykes. The Glitch has been known to cancel bills outright, to record payments that were never made, to erase overdue sums of money, and to misdirect bills to someone who can afford to pay them. It is She who "bugs" computers, causing them to become "down" at times most inconvenient to the patriarchs. We need The Glitch in our lives, for She promises a multitude of joy to those Dykes who know which buttons to push.

The casual observance of the rites of Digitalis may be enacted by fingering materials of any kind, twiddling one's thumbs, or pointing a finger. She abhors those who chew or "bite" their fingernails "down to the nub," but Her followers are known to engage in a ritual of Trimming which, they say, increases their pleasure in Rubbing. Her sacred numbers are 5 and 10, and She can always be counted upon. These are touchy subjects.

DOLORES, sometimes invoked as La Dolorosa, is our goddess of grief and mourning. Hers is a benign and nurturing influence, for She teaches us that grief, like joy, is both necessary and transient. To experience one is to open the doors of be-ing to the other. It is She who guides us as we give voice to the depths of our sorrow and pain of any kind, be it the loss of a loved one or the ability to trust after violence or abuse, or the end of a relationship in which we've grown and flourished. Initiates new to the whelming experience of grief frequently make great claims for Dolores, asserting that She must be a major goddess among Lesbians. Indeed, there may be truth in what they say because Lesbians experience so many losses during our stay on Earth, where change and transience are inevitable. Many Lesbians lose the love of their families and friends when they reveal their identity. Others repeatedly experience the pain of ended or changed relationships, a cycle perpetuated by the Blaming Ritual, during which first one, then the other friend or lover, Places the Blame for the end on the other Lesbian. Although many Lesbians mistakenly perform this ritual in the belief that it will erase or suppress their pain, this is an illusion, for Blaming simply feeds the pain, allowing it to fester and endure. Grieving and mourning our changes and losses, the Blessings of Dolores, enable us to cherish the good things in all our relationships, and to appreciate the ways we can learn from pain as well as joy.

All endings are sacred to Dolores, for they signal beginnings in all things. If something ends, surely a new door in life is about to open. Grieving readies us to walk through each door, so time and care must be given to that process. Trying to ignore our pain strengthens its hold on us, so that we carry it with us into places where it doesn't belong. Worse, refusing to mourn an ending will give it power over our future actions.

There is no pain too small for Dolores to attend to, and there are many ways to seek Her nurturing embrace. When the feelings of a friend or lover have changed, and you wish to acknowledge the pain of your loss, repeat one of the following incantations, whichever seems appropriate for your feelings.

> Kind Dolores, I acknowledge my pain;
> Help me to grieve without anger or blame.

> Dolores, she who loved me well is gone.
> I will pour out my grief, loud and long.

> I mourn, Dolores, yet another end;
> Help me to grieve for the loss of my friend.

Uttering these and similar incantations is known to be both soothing and useful, for they enable us to acknowledge the significance of the companion, animal or person, in our lives, and give voice to the pain we experience when we're separated from those we cherish. When we love well, we must also grieve well, lest we slight the love that meant much to us.

Whenever we find ourselves in pain, Dolores is there, She understands, and helps us to journey through it. The well-known phrase, "Good Grief," acknowledges the healing power of grieving fully and well.

DOMICILA, the goddess of Lesbian dwellings, gets us where we live. She is worshipped in two ritual cycles, not to be confused with bi-cycles. The first cycle begins with The Hunt, in which participants follow cryptic clues to find The Perfect Place. These clues are often found in sacred documents known as the Classified Ads, although the significance of this name is now lost to us. One scholar, after pouring over countless sheets of these ads, has speculated that they may be called "Classified" after the fashion in which their compilers sought to "classify" them, sorting them into a variety of types, sometimes based on compass directions or the kind of dwelling involved. This is, of course, merely speculation, but she points convincingly to one distinction that appears frequently, that between "For Sale"and "For Rent." Another hypothesis advanced by some experts suggests that these documents, because of the mysterious codes and the exceedingly fine type used to print them, are called "Classified" because of the esoteric and highly secret nature of their content. (Some translations of this code are offered below.) Further study will doubtless reveal the significance of other aspects of the Classified Ads as well.

Initiates into the obscure mysteries of Domicila are known to pore over the Classifieds with great devotion and intensity, and they become adept at interpreting the meaning of phrases such as "cozy" (which means 'tiny'), "quiet neighborhood" (meaning: 'no partying'), "Landlord (or manager) on premises" (meaning: 'don't live here if you like privacy'), "historic building" (meaning: 'is falling down'), "gracious living" (meaning: 'you can't afford it'), "access to highways" (meaning: 'the Interstate runs through the front yard'), "quaint four-story" (meaning: 'no elevators'), and "lovely view" (meaning: 'all you can see from your windows is the building next door'). These elaborate, often deceptive codes, are thought to have been literal at some stage in the past, but we've dis-covered no evidence that supports this idea.

At this point, we must caution those who wish to attempt a Reading of the Classified Ads. It has been brought to our attention that such Readings have been known to cause a disease, called Smudges, on the hands of participants. We have it on good authority that Smudges reproduces and spreads quickly, appearing spontaneously on foreheads, noses, and cheeks in mere seconds after contact. We do not yet know how dangerous Smudges is.

Having successfully found their way through the Classifieds, completion of The Hunt is followed by the rituals of The Closing or Signing the Lease, and then Moving In, an arduous test of strength, endurance, and self-control which Domicila shares with **MARIA'**.

The second cycle includes such rites as Hanging the Posters, Decorating, Warming the House, Planting the Garden, Mowing the Lawn, Shoveling the Walk, Painting, Filling the Waterbed, and Cleaning the Toilet, depending on the individual needs and purposes of the celebrants. These comprise an endless cycle of rituals and observances known as Dyke Domesticity, which necessitate the cooperation of **LABOREA** and **CHEMIA** as well.

Devotees of Domicila generally are considered to form two

37

groups, based upon their preference for one or the other of Her ritual cycles. Some prefer the second cycle, and settle into the routines of Dyke Domesticity, including in their lives regular observances devoted to related goddesses such as Chemia and Laborea, in Her Kitchen Witch aspect. Others find the greatest satisfaction in Her first ritual cycle, which they celebrate by moving with every seasonal change, to the great dismay of their friends and those who maintain our mailing lists.

ELECTRA charges the many ways we gynergetically spark, and is known to us in many aspects: all are Electrafying! One of these, AMANA, is said to be AC-DC, for Her love of Current Events. Her attributes—toasters, typewriters, washing machines, and refrigerators—collectively known as Appliances in all their models, are often turned on during observances sacred to **LABOREA**, COLLATEA, **DOMICILA**, and **MUNCHIES**, but some Dykes avoid such rituals, saying they are turned off. Shrines to Amana, called Laundramats, contain rows of altars, where, for an offering of currency, devotees enact Her rituals, The Wash and Rinse Cycles. The Gynergetics celebrate the Spin Cycle as Electra's most sacred rite, wherefore they are also called Spinsters. Another aspect, known affectionately to Her initiates as GE, short for Get Even, is said to Have a Better Idea.

Electra frequently arrives exuberantly in outlets called Power Surges, and some thearists suggest a connection to **DIGITALIS** as a consequence. She runs well, even on batteries, and abhors the fathers' false distinction between "work" and "play." Where energy abounds, there She will be! Electra goes with the flow, and Her devotees, it is said, are always wired. MEDIA is sometimes called the "Fair to Middling" aspect of Electra for Her visible habit of Plugging Products during Her frequent Commercial Breaks, short glorifications to a host of goddesses, among them: AMANA, OXYDOLY, BONA AMIA, COCA-COLA, LONG JANE SILVER's, JILL-IN-THE-BOX, and PALM OLIVIA.

Pondering the mysteries of Amana

When one of Her priestesses chants, "And now a Word from Our Sponsor," devotees of this aspect of Electra rise as one from their seats of observation and hasten to their refrigerators, washers, dryers, or even, in tight situations, to **EVACUA's** porcelain shrines. When Media accepts their diverse offerings, and responds with the words "Be There!," they are said to be Tuned In or On the Right Channel.

Electra isn't picky about Her observances, and some invoke Her Presence by Playing Instruments on the altars, called Turn Tables, of one of Her lesser aspects, OLIVIA, who, it is recorded, keeps on turning. These devotees can be heard vying for Electra's blessings on the Day and Night Stages at Her annual observances, called "music festivals." Thousands of worshippers gather at these events staged in Electra's name, traveling miles under the guidance of **ASPHALTA** and Her Flagwimmin. Once arrived, they consume great quantities of peanut butter, honey, and cantaloupes, washing them down with cold showers. Shrines to Evacua, called Porta-Janes, dot the landscape, and invocations to **CUDDLES**, **NEMEHA'ALISH**, and **LILIHA'ALA'A** are often mouthed as old friends hug and new friends sing the hymn to Olivia, "Let's Get Lesbian."

VIDEA, whose many altars—videa games and pinball machines—can be found in dark shrines called Arcadia, favors those with many tokens, small disks that symbolize our larger circles. These tokens must be "properly inserted" into small openings called "slots." Failure to properly insert a token into an altar must be followed immediately with a swift kick or banging fist. Videa loves these caresses, and will often respond by rewarding Her devotee with a "Free Game." She frowns on those who Tilt, and they lose their turn. Those who incur Her wrath get the message "Game Over," and the only way they can continue their worship is by inserting more sacred disks into Her slots. Among the more esoteric aspects of Videa are QWIX, FROGGA, PACWOMON, CENTIPEDA, and the more arcane MILLIPEDA.

The Presence of Electra is centrally-aired in so many spheres of Dyke Endeavor that some re-searchers suggest She may be Our Goddess of Tools. They support this claim by pointing to Her efficient aspects, Appliances, found in spaces sacred to Domicila, the Power Tools employed by tradeswomyn, and the Instruments used to worship Olivia, as well as those hand-held in rituals to VIBRATA. Skeptics charge that this sounds good as long as She's running well, but remind us that She is more and more frequently given to Brown Outs and Black Outs, when candles must be lit to appease Her. Although the undercurrents in this debate are neither alternating nor direct, they generate great friction.

ET CETERA, She-Who-Takes-Much-For-Granted, defends the indefensible and envelopes the unspecified and the unspecifiable, those things and ideas that clutter our lives with nuisance and frustration. She attends to all the details we prefer to gloss over. Wherefore Her sacred abbreviation, ETC., is often added at the end of tiresomely long lists in irrelevant and boring contexts, for it symbolizes that All-We-Have-Not-Said falls under Her protection. One of Her most esoteric invocations, called the CYA (Cover Your Ass), is thought by many to be a wise move. A CYA must remain unspecified.

Et Cetera is often called upon when Lesbians wish to take something like consent or consensus for granted, invite other Lesbians to join them in the thrift shop of ideology, ETC. She wastes no time Spelling Things Out, Tying Up Loose Ends, ETC., so She is frequently invoked when **ANOMIA** causes us to lose a word temporarily, and to Her are attributed those Doodads, Thingamajigs, Whatchamacallits, Whoozymawhatzits, Thingamabobs, and So-And-Sos so frequent in our speech. Properly intoned, any one of these will suffice as a CYA. Et Cetera can also be called upon to fill an awkward moment by saying "Ya Know" after every other word. So versatile is "Ya Know" that adepts claim that subtle variations in intonation can suggest myriad possible interpretations. "Ya Know," it is said, can mean almost anything.

A contemporary mis-spelling of Her sacred abbreviation

43

continues to spread—ECT.—an unlovely reversal and prof-
anation. Many of Et Cetera's hopeful initiates, thinking to
invoke Her with ECT., have been disappointed, then re-
morseful when, awakening from their ritual trance,
they've found themselves surrounded by ectomorphs and
ectoderms. (Ectoderms are rare, eight-sided elephants
found only in transcendent realities. They are known to be
pesky and cantankerous if invoked In Error.)

Et Cetera's symbol is the Ampersand (&, &tc.), & those
who flounder among Her Whoozits and Whatchamacallits
are said to chant monotonously, "ETC., ETC., ETC., ETC.,
ETC., ETC.," and find, thereby, some measure of infinity,
ETC.

Her Prayer Wheel

**ETC., ETC., ETC., ETC., ETC., ETC., ETC., ETC.,
ETC., ETC., ETC., ETC., ETC., ETC., ETC., ETC.,
ETC., ETC., ETC., ETC., ETC., ETC. ,ETC., ETC.,
ETC., ETC., ETC., ETC., ETC., ETC., ETC., ETC.,
ETC., ETC., ETC., ETC., ETC., ETC., ETC., ETC.,
ETC., ETC., ETC., ETC., ETC., ETC., ETC., ETC.,
ETC., ETC., ETC., ETC., ETC., ETC., ETC., ETC.,
ETC., ETC., ETC., ETC., ETC., ETC., ETC., ETC.,
ETC., ETC., ETC., ETC., ETC., ETC., ETC., ETC.,
ETC., ETC., ETC., ETC., ETC., ETC., ETC., ETC.,
ETC., ETC., ETC., ETC., ETC., ETC., ETC., ETC.,
ETC., ETC., ETC., ETC., ETC., ETC., ETC., ETC.,
ETC., ETC., ETC., ETC., ETC., ETC., ETC., ETC.,
ETC., ETC., ETC., ETC., ETC., ETC., ETC., ETC.,
ETC., ETC., ETC., ETC., ETC., ETC., ETC., ETC.,
ETC., ETC., ETC., ETC., ETC., ETC., ETC., ETC.,
ETC., ETC., ETC.,......**

EUPHORIA, the goddess of intense, but transient pleasures, is Sister to the goddesses **CUDDLES**, **LILI-HA'ALA'A**, **NEMEHA'ALISH**, **CHOCOLATA**, **CHAN-CY** (yes! Her Presence can be invoked even at potlucks!), **DEA ABLEA**, **HILARIA**, and both **CHEMIA** and **DE-TOXIA**. The rituals which call forth all of these and others frequently bring Euphoria bubbling and giggling into our midst. Wherever Dykes are gathered together in the celebration of themselves, a smile, a touch, a burst of raucous laughter suffices to call Euphoria to our sides. There are many Paths to the Presence of Euphoria, and those who seek Her with the senses of their bodies and the passions of their minds always find Her. As a companion to OR-GASMIA, Euphoria takes special delight in the spasms, jerks, and strenuous outcries that herald Orgasmia's arrival in our midsts.

It is important to note here that Euphoria doesn't *do* anything Herself—sacred to Her are those fleeting "states of mind," unmapped, unlimited by the boundaries of patriarchy, which we create through our own pleasures. Today, many Dykes associate Euphoria with certain chemical changes in their brains, and they report feelings of Light-headedness, Dizzy-ness, and intense well-Be-ing. Lesbians of all sorts have come to know Euphoria well, and seek the pleasures of Her rituals and revel-ations whenever and wherever possible.

The Presence of Euphoria is sometimes symbolized by the

45

Doe, who appears suddenly and fleetingly at the edge of our minds' forests and disappears as quickly, melting back into the protective shadows of Her Domain.

However we may choose to invoke the Presence of Euphoria, She is always among us, and chooses Her Own Moments. Many seek Her, many find Her, but none can hold Her for long.

Dea Ablea

EUTOPIA/DYSTOPIA, the two-faced goddess of all Lesbian visions, attends music festivals, poetry readings, collective meetings, concerts, rap groups, and potlucks, where She is in charge of atmosphere. The ritual observances sacred to Eutopia/Dystopia are called For-ums because the priestesses who facilitate these meetings, when asked why they bother, retreat into mystery, responding, "It's for...um...um...."

At these celebrations, Eutopia/Dystopia is invoked when the Topic of the For-um is announced. The Topics must be specific enough to spark heated discussion, but sufficiently vague to give Eutopia/Dystopia latitude for deciding which of Her faces will show. They are chosen from the Current Slate of Issues. Old favorites include: monogamy/non-monogamy, sado-masochism, racism, classism, roles, ageism, sizeism, looksism, Separatism, and able-bodied-ism. The priestesses who volunteer to facilitate these For-ums open the celebration by intoning the Pros and Cons of the ritual Topic while the celebrants collect thoughts, and then voice opinions. These are offered whether or not the priestesses ask for them. Eutopia is said to grace a gathering where there is no conflict or where there is conflict resolution. Dystopia is said to manifest Herself where there is heated argument, confrontation, and dissent into chaos. Skeptics maintain that Dystopia prefers the façade of agreement, a false sense of well-being. It is Eutopia who savors honest opposition and energetic discord. Some say that one opinion is as good as another. Others disagree.

Of some significance is a tendency, noted by astute observers, for devotees of Eutopia/Dystopia to invoke only Her benign aspect, ignoring Dystopia altogether. They claim that, by focusing their energy on the "good feelings" generated by Eutopian revel-ations, they dis-spell **QUIETUS**.

Others, however, remarking on the charms of Dystopia, regard this focus as Out of Line, a serious mis-spelling. These devotees of Eutopia/Dystopia, calling themselves The PC's (The Purely Collective), believe the emphasis on Eutopia derives from addictive practices typical of rituals to **EUPHORIA**, **CHEMIA**, and **DEA ABLEA**, observances reputed to induce Euphoric Highs among the indulgent.

At least one thearist notes that obsessive invocations to Eutopia, and denial of Her dual facets, reveal, not the proper observance of Her essence, but the distorted perceptions more typical of followers of **POLLYANNA**, She-Who-Fogs-the-Mind. Some support for this comparison can be found in the Eutopian habit of mind, called CLING-FREE, where there is no static. Harping eternally on the ec-static, these PI's (Pure Individuals) say that Eutopia's Presence is "felt" during Lesbian gatherings that "go well," and they speak wistfully of such rituals and a sense of "well-be-ing" that quell their dis-ease. Much of this may well be relative, for only a few Gatherings can be said to "go well," and Dystopia is far more likely to appear than Eutopia, no matter who is invoked by the celebrants. Why are we surprised?

Perennial devotees of Eutopia/Dystopia and Her festivities claim to have spotted the goddess PLETHORA skirting is-

48

sues at mass observances, such as the Michigan Womyn's Music Festival. Plethora is a late bloomer, but, they say, "When it rains, it pours," and Plethora smiles giddily on teems and influxes. She is Abundance in All Things, and is said to be hyperactive in Hart. This, perhaps, explains why so many goddesses converge when Eutopia/Dystopia is invoked.

Is it design or coincidence that such diverse Be-ings as Polyanna, Euphoria, Chemia, **DETOXIA**, **PYROMANIA**, and even Dea Ablea have been known to invite themselves to the noisy revel-ations of Eutopia/Dystopia? Although the WWTMC claims to limit revelling to One Significant Issue at their annual observances, Plethora will not be dampened, and each year's issues proliferate like workshops at a wimmin's conference. Sometimes participants have been known to Dance Around an Issue through the night, and those who return from these strenuous rituals relate at great length the Pros and the Cons of This Issue and That Issue, swearing they have looked upon both of Eutopia/Dystopia's faces at once.

Faithful devotees, who strain their budgets to attend these rituals, maintain that there are no coincidences in this world or any other, claiming that such complex associations of so many Found Goddesses merely point to the obvious: that all goddesses are One-in-the-Many, and cannot be separated One from the Other. Some go so far as to say that it is the work of Quietus to distinguish The Goddess as though She had specialized, and assert that classifications of all kinds are patriarchal deceptions.

Under Plethora's influence, some Lesbians committed to revel-ing and revel-ation believe that **any** occasion is cause enough to celebrate, and they have been known to *make* *up their own goddesses* in order to Party Down. Such an event is called a *cause célèbre*. Some regard this practice as tasteless, while others lustily proclaim "The More the Better" as a Primary Principle.

However individual Lesbians choose to worship Eutopia/Dystopia, Pyromania, The Burning One, is certainly closely-related. We can safely assert this as a Truth because so many devotees of Eutopia/Dystopia eventually seek the warmth of Pyromania, calling upon Her after an exhaustive and too-long Gathering. A few seek the serenity of **INERTIA** and are never heard from again.

EVACUA, too frequently regarded as an insignificant, minor goddess and shunned by some, who, alas, are embarrassed by Her profusions, is often evoked for succor and comfort during difficult or painful processes, such as coming out, working one's way through a creative block, struggling to achieve a collective decision, or seeking clarity in a multitude of situations and conflicts. Evacua also bestows relief from a variety of intestinal and bowel discomforts. Diarrhea and Constipia are two of Her many aspects, and they are difficult, like so many of our Passages and Processes, but they are necessary physical revel-ations of overflow or blockage. Her priestesses are rightly known for their Intestinal Fortitude. In all of Her aspects, Evacua is a primary goddess of Lesbians and, doubtless, many of our contemporary problems can be traced to our ignorance and neglect of Her rites. We must learn to spell R-E-L-I-E-F with the proper reverence.

One of Her most regarded aspects, called DEB, (short for DYKES EVER BOUNDING), is worshipped in high-falutin' all-night rituals called Debutante Bawls,* annual events that celebrate the beginning of the process known as Coming Out. During these rituals, every new Dyke is reverently welcomed into the Community, and her defiance of the fathers is acclaimed by much hootin' and hollerin', for she has found her Voice. Noise, it is said, is much loved by every aspect of Evacua, but especially by DEB. Indeed, these noises are so significant in Her worship that devotees often bring along one or several Sacred Cows to the festivities, for they add moos to the revelry. One Crone researcher has suggested that these Coming Out rituals are called "Bawls" because, at some dim point in time, our Sacred Cows were actually sacrificed as offerings to DEB, but we've been unable to find hide nor hair to support this claim.

Months before one of these ritual extravaganzas, the Dykes of a Community can be found attending minor, preliminary rites called Rummage Sales, where they vie with each other to purchase moth-eaten tuxedos and old prom dresses. These items of apparel are essential to the success of a Debutante Bawl, and they must be *used*, for they symbolize the Act of Discarding (or Shedding) the false selves created by the fathers' lies. Thus, in their more esoteric interpretation, these old outfits also represent the Dyke Un-Doing of patriarchal re-versals and a return to one's true Self.

A Debutante Bawl begins when one of DEB's priestesses yells "Come Out, Come Out, wherever you are!," and the Dyke Novices come running from every direction. They respond to her invitation by chanting in unison, "I'm Coming, I'm Coming," and throwing off their garments symbolizing their Old Selves. When this phase is completed, all the participants join together in a great snake, and dance joyfully to the tune, "Sherry, Can You Come Out Tonight?" This is called the DEB Dance, but we have been unable to dis-cover who "Sherry" was or if she ever Came Out. So much has been lost to us.

Exhausted by the exertions of the DEB Dance, the celebrants sit, squat, or lie in a circle on the floor, cushioned by the piles of tuxedos and prom dresses, and the next phase of the ritual begins, Telling Tales. These may be short or tall, but all are recited under the auspices of HY-PERBOLE, She-Who-Gives-Tongue. Each initiate tells her Coming Out Story, usually with much embellishment, exaggeration, and pride, as she wishes it to be re-membered in Oral Herstory. So e-motive is this stage of the Bawl that other goddesses, notably **DOLORES** and **HILARIA**, often join the circle, spreading both weeping and laughter as the initiates celebrate the pain and pleasure of their processes. Often, one cannot be distinguished from the other, and much noise is raised.

After the healing of this sharing, the initiates are liberally massaged with great quantities of vegetable oil, signifying their connection to Mother Earth. The other celebrants then line up with their legs spread, making a tunnel, and the initiates slide through this tunnel, often with the help and support of many hands, until they have passed through. Some passages are easy, others are difficult, but each arrives at her own pace. This phase of the ritual represents the initiates' self-creation, the support of their new Dyke Community, and the E-mergence of their Dyke Selves.

When each initiate has come out of the tunnel, she is proclaimed a Dyke, for she has begun her life again. These revel-ations to DEB may last for weeks, even months, but when they end each celebrant gathers up her discarded clothes for she keeps them as beloved tokens of her Old Self. No Dyke can disclaim her former selves.

Because Lesbians are constantly changing our minds and shapes, we sometimes evoke Evacua as She-Who-Shines-in-

Mistakes. As Alix Dobkin, a Crone and Bard, has wisely said, "Lesbians are getting good at one thing: Making mistakes!" Because we should take pride in all our accomplishments, and be kind to ourselves, we must applaud those things in which we excel, especially the TRIVIA-L. We're getting better and better at the making of mistakes, and Evacua, sometimes mistakenly assumed to be an opposing aspect of **INERTIA**, cherishes all of them.

It is Evacua who oversees our painful transitions and hard passages, easing the way for those who sincerely call upon Her. When you think you can't stand whatever it is you're going through for one more moment, find a bathroom. Her shrines are everywhere and called by many sacred names—The Restroom, The Powder Room, The Ladies' Room, The Necessary Room, or, simply, Hers. Visiting one of these shrines is sometimes called, "Taking a Powder." If you're camping or back-packing when you realize it's time to invoke Evacua, go off by yourself. Privacy is essential for proper evocation.

Feel free, once alone in your meditation, to squeeze a roll of toilet paper as you call upon the benevolence of Evacua. Inhale and exhale as deeply and sincerely as you can. Continue breathing deeply until you feel the sure signs of Evacua's Presence, abdominal relaxation as tension flows out of your body. Now, inhale until your lungs are full. As your lungs begin to ache for release, curl your tongue so that the edges just touch your upper teeth (or gums) and hold the tip right behind your upper teeth (or gums), and force the air from your lungs through the narrow opening between your tongue and teeth (or gums) in one long, uninterrupted scream: "S-S-S-S-S-H-H-H-H-I-I-I-I-I-I-I-I-I-I-I-I-T-T-T-T-T-T-T...." Prolong this evocation as long as your retained air holds out, the longer and louder the better. Southern

Dykes are said to excel beyond all others in the prolongation of this evocation.

Less well-known aspects of Evacua—TUMS, ROLAIDS, and ALKA-SELTZER—are goddesses of belches and burps, indulgences only recently re-discovered by contemporary Dykes researching the roots of the Old Religion. The sacred practices of Belching and Burping have long been taboo observances under the rule of the fathers, but we're learning, once again, to savor the culinary memories they bespeak. A Lesbian burping or belching, especially in public, where many can hear her lusty evocation, is said to be Rude, Crude, and Socially Unacceptable, which is the highest praise Evacua can bestow on a devotee. Belching, Burping, and especially Farting, are regarded as sure signs of Her blessing, and signify, for all to hear (or smell) a Bad Attitude.

Evacua cherishes our exertions in Her Name and, when properly evoked, many say that the appearance of Evacua is often followed by **EUPHORIA**. Remember, you are evoking She-Who-Guards-Our-Passages. Let it all out!!! Evacua will hear!

---

*These celebrations are said to have been in-spired by Willie Tyson's song, *Debutante Ball*, and her album *Debutante* (Urana Records, 1977), the jacket of which features Willie attired in a tuxedo accompanied by a meditative cow.

FALLOPIA watches over the physical cycles of wimmin's lives. Her periodic rituals celebrate both the manifest—puberty, menstruation, and menopause—and the covert—Saturn returns, biorhythms, and Moon Days. Although Her appearances are frequently irregular, Her devotees assure Her Presence in their lives when they carry symbols of Her power—pads, tampons and sponges, which they often wear as earrings, bracelets, and broaches. When they adorn themselves with Her symbols they say She is Always with them.

Some eschew such obvious attempts to coax Fallopia's beneficence, but Her followers Rely upon demonstrations of their love, which they say is Sure and Natural. Not all of Her aspects are pleasant, and many wimmin find Her periodic visitations dread-ful. Because experiencing Her splendor may be accompanied by pains known as "cramps," many evoke **EVACUA** to remove these blocks to full experience of Fallopia.

It is from the tradition of Fallopia that we derive the phrase "to see red," which originally referred to the perceptual changes we experience during Her menstrual observances. More recently, though, this phrase has been generalized to refer to the profound anger that many wimmin feel when they comprehend the extent of their oppression under the rule of the fathers.

These irregular perceptual shifts prepare us gradually for

one of the most important celebrations in our lives, Meno-pause, when we cease to count our years in terms of the "monthlies." This observance, which can last anywhere from five to ten years, is of such magnitude and significance that it is often simply referred to as "The Change." During Menopause, wimmin experience sudden visitations of Fallopia, called "Hot Flashes," which they regard as spiritual revel-ations. Some of these flashes are intense, others are fleeting, but each marks Fallopia's Presence. Following the transformational experience that is The Change, a womon is said to be Croned. Blessed are the Haggard!*

Because the practice of counting and the discovery of numbers arose as part of the ritual observances to Fallopia, when wimmin kept track of their menstrual cycles by carving lines on bones in the shape of quarter moons, Fallopia is also the special guardian of the realm of Mathematica, an abstract consciousness sought by those wimmin who call themselves Mathematicians. These are said to dwell forever in the realm of whole and unreal numbers, where they seek their square roots.

One of Fallopia's monthly observances, dis-covered by the vibrant Virago, Sally Gearhart, is called Singing the Eggs Down,** when celebrants invoke Her as CILIA, The Wave-Maker, so called because of the waves of ecstasy that signal the successful release of each egg. As each egg begins its journey to the womb, participants call out, "Is it Ova yet?" a question held by some to be unanswerable and, therefore, profoundly obscure.

Fallopia, because of Her disposition, is also held to be responsible for vaginitis and yeast infections, and wimmin seeking relief from these visitations make frequent offerings of yogurt and vinegar in order to rid themselves of "the itch that cannot be scratched." Fallopia is renowned for Her acerbic wit.

---

*For further information about Crones and the Haggard, see *Gyn/Ecology* by Mary Daly, (Boston: Beacon Press, 1978), 15-16.
**Sally Gearhart, *The Wanderground* (Boston: Alyson Publications, 1984).

GETTUFFA is Our-Goddess-of-Self-Defense, She-Who-Kicks-Quick, and She is known for Her proud stance and wide stride. She moves through time in split-seconds, be-ing neither Here nor There yet always Wherever, Whenever a Dyke calls upon Her in anger or distress. Her visage is said to be disarming. It is Her Name we call when men harass us on the street or at work, in any circumstances in which we feel threatened with violence or harm, physical or emotional. Because Gettuffa is often invoked at the Last Minute when time is short, many devotees use a chopped form of Her Name, TUFFA, for these syllables slip easily through clenched teeth, erupting in sharp grunts and harsh gasps:

> Tuffa, Tuffa, chop, block, leap;
> Help me decimate this creep.

Tuffa supports us in our struggles to become strong and swift, and She is frequently worshipped in dojos and womyn's self-defense classes, where initiates learn the mysteries of Sparring and Blocking. The priestesses who conduct these classes are called *Guðwēne*, ('Battle Queen', a term of great respect used during the Golden Age among the Amazons of Albion).* She may be invoked in any of Her several aspects—Karate, Tae Kwon Do, Tai Chi, Aikido, and Judo—and Her observances are called the Martial Arts. Because these offensive and defensive rituals are often performed on floor coverings called "mats," Gettuffa's hair is reputed to be so matted that it resembles a tangle of angry snakes.

Her devotees are much given to cries and howls, noises cherished by **EVACUA**, as they whirl and spin. It is said she rejoices in the flowing sweat that drenches the bodies of the Exerted, for she who works out becomes a Tuff Dyke, capable of defending herself against those who would do her harm. When several Tuff Dykes wrestle together upon a mat, laughing and shrieking, this is called a *mǣdenhēap* (literally, "pile of warriors," after the Amazons of Albion in the Golden Age).*

GETTUFFA

Because Dykes live surrounded by danger, Gettuffa responds readily to a variety of invocations, from the thoughtfully elaborate to the tersely immediate.

> Come, Gettuffa, let my aim be true;
> This prick's preying days are through!

> Hey Gettuffa! I'm being hounded;
> When I fight back, they'll be confounded!

Because it is She who encourages us to act in situations of danger, some invocations are more strenuous than others. When threatened and outnumbered, some Tuff Dykes quickly cry out:

> Jab and poke! Stab and chop!
> Kick the pricks till they drop!

One Tuff Dyke chant, said to be particularly effective when intoned in a threatening, throaty snarl by a group of Lesbians, has been known to drive men from the streets. Its simplicity strikes at the source of male presumption. As you walk down the street, chant loudly and repeatedly,

> Wither and fall off,
> Wither and fall off,
> Wither and fall off....

On and on. "They" will know exactly what you mean! This invocation to Gettuffa was once known far and wide, but seems to have fallen into disuse in these latter days as righteous anger has been suppressed and denied. One of the fiercest aspects of Gettuffa, KILLAMAN, is all but lost to us, but our strenuous re-searching re-vealed one of Her most powerful invocations:

61

> Killaman, Killaman! Spirit of Frenzy,
> Stand beside me, rise within me!

A protective spell, said to surround the Tuff Dyke with an angry aura guaranteed to frighten any presumptuous male, can be addressed directly to the wrong-doer who is threatening you:

> I'll Gettuffa and say it true:
> I don't want to deal with you.

A strong stance and a can of mace are also helpful. GET-TUFFA!

---

*See note at end of **CUDDLES** for references to Wittig and Zeig's *Lesbian Peoples*; for information on Old English mǣdenhēap and other lost words, see "*Woman and Wife* : Social and Semantic Shifts in English," Julia Penelope (Stanley) and Cynthia McGowan, in *Papers in Linguistics* 12, 3-4 (1979), esp. 500.

HILARIA, undoubtedly one of the most widely acknowledged and revered of the the Found Goddesses, is always good for a laugh. With Her rib-tickling companions, CHUCKLES, CHORTLES, GIGGLES and GUFFAWS, She is invoked in diverse circumstances with varying degrees of success, for much depends upon the intentions of those Who seek Her. She abhors the nervous TITTERS, associated with GAMEY (see **UMPIRA** and **VISCERA**), but is easily summoned by the lusty laughter often heard at **CHANCY**'s potlucks or COLLATEA's (see **LABOREA**) rituals. Especially dear to Her are those known for their Wicked Laughs, and She listens lovingly to the cackles that rise like suddenly freed birds from the throats of encircled Crones.

One of Hilaria's best-known rituals is Humor Control, used to bring the participants closer together, by emphasizing their shared experiences, or to lighten tense or hostile situations. Because Her Presence enables us to get through so many intolerable situations and painful confrontations, She is especially dear to Lesbians, who frequently engage in the ritual of Humor Control. Hilaria may be invoked informally by saying, "If I don't laugh, I'll cry," or by using one of Her formal invocations for making light*, such as:

> Hail Hilaria, Mother Wit,
> We can't stand all this shit.
> Haggle, gaggle, wiggle, and wag,
> Bless us with a joke or a gag.

She is much given to the Rite of Tongue in Cheek, and, in Her medicinal aspect, will leave Her devotees in stitches. If the situation calls for uproarious hilarity, she may be invoked by chanting:

> Hail Hilaria, do your bit,
> Bring us laughter, soul of Wit!

or,

> Wholly Hilaria, silly and daft,
> Truly you know we need a good laugh!

Humor Control must be a consensual activity, for much depends upon the appropriateness of the aspect of Hilaria invoked and how well the participants know each other. Her priestesses teach that timing and sensitivity are all when Her Presence is sought, for there are many touchy subjects among us. Caution must be urged when invoking Hilaria, for an aura of mutual trust among the devotees is essential to the ritual of Humor Control. Where it does not exist, Hilaria cannot be summoned, and the only result will be increased tensions and hostility. To call upon Her as a diversion from serious struggle or out of a desire for attention isn't laughable, for Hilaria doesn't fool around. The demon of false laughter, TEE HEE, smirking and leering, thrives in an atmosphere of mistrust.

Some re-searchers claim that Hilaria has an ecstatic aspect they call HYSTERIA, or She-of-the-Rumbling Womb, and they attribute to Her the womb-laughter that rises up, wave upon wave, so powerful that its thunderous bursts cause every part of our bodies to shake and quiver with its release. They support this claim by reminding us that Hysteria is a State of Awareness only wimmin can attain, and thearize that patriarchal attempts to suppress Her outbursts by calling them "irrational" (origins unknown), reveals how dangerous and empowering Her influence is. Much remains to be dis-covered about the healing power of womb-laughter.

Hilaria's sacred covens are called Glee Clubs, where Her initiates gather to laugh up sleeves and split seams, making offerings to Her of Funny Money, borrowed without interest. Her color is yellow, and, where Her symbol the Happy Face is found, there is said to be much Gaiety, an observance rooted in ancient practices sacred to the lost goddess, GAIA.

---

*For more examples of making light, hear Kate Clinton's album, *Making Light* (WhysCrack Records, POB 291989, Los Angeles, CA 90029) and read her article, "Making Light: Notes on Feminist Humor" in *Trivia* 1 (Fall, 1982, p. 37+). Also relevant to Hilaria is Be-Laughing, as Pronounced in Mary Daly's *The Wickedary*, Appendicular Web Two, 261-72.

INERTIA and EXERTIA are the twin goddesses who embody the sacred dual principle which holds that bodies in motion stay in motion, while bodies at rest tend to remain at rest. These are Great Mysteries indeed. Some adherents of Inertia take the Path of Least Resistance, while others never get started at all. These say that the rituals of Exertia are excessive and tiring. The feline species (see **ANIMA**) is held to be especially dear to Inertia/Exertia and all those who do not exert influence because cats are either "in motion" or "motion-less."

Those who doubt the sister relationship between Inertia and Exertia would do well to remark those wimmin who continue to work and work and work in the Move-ment despite advanced Burn-Out (see **PYROMANIA**), and those who claim they have been "carried away" by passion in any of its varied forms. (Of the latter, it is not known where they are "taken" or whether they return, if they do.) Such wimmin, filled with the e-motions of de-votion, keep themselves frantically in motion without being moved. Consumed by Exertia's compulsion, these wimmin constantly drive themselves. So ignited are they by the idea of "staying in motion" that they often end up "spinning wheels," going nowhere. Working at Stick Shifts too hard and too long, the ritual observances of Exertia often lead to Inertia.

Other wimmin, aware of Exertia's dead ends, have been known to devote their entire lives to the observances of Inertia, and they are much given to the ritual of R & R, Rest and Relaxation, idling their time away. It is said they indulge frequently in idle conversation and cherish their "spare time," claiming it as the special gift of Inertia. Her priestesses can be readily identified by their sacred habit of Flaking Out.

Among Inertia's most sacred observances is the Rite of Procrastination, during which Her followers adopt horizontal attitudes and prone positions in motion-less vehicles called "reclining chairs," where they invoke Her by lolling about. Truly, it is said, "Blessed are they who Procrastinate, for they toil not, neither do they overdo nor do they stress out. Verily, they shall live to see Cronehood."

Inertia has been known to fluctuate in Her moods, a characteristic which links Her definitively with the Lunatic Fringe. These devotees travel in large groups, called Influxes, to music festivals, where they lie prone in lounge chairs at great length. Her symbol is the Lollipop, which, it is claimed, gives succor to Her worshippers, but All-Day Suckers also pacify Her.

Inertia's shrines are conveniently located, and She shares those temples to **EVACUA** called "Restrooms." Inertia has many aspects worshipped in our dwellings, including SOFA, DIVANA, and SETTEE. Love Seats are often found where Lesbians gather to celebrate the rituals sacred to **LILIHA'ALA'A** and **CUDDLES**.

At rest or in motion, it is generally acknowledged that Inertia/Exertia can be a helpful goddess, although Her observances can also be very demanding. They can enhance as well as prevent growth and change, and either Path can lead to stag-nation.

IOTA, Our Mother of the Minute, Protector of the Petite, isn't accorded the proper reverence among some Lesbians, who point to Her Negligible Influence, and the habit of Her priestesses, who invoke Her by proclaiming, "I won't give an Iota!" Her devotees, however, regard such attitudes as petty, maintaining that this perception reveals a sizeist bias against smallness. Her initiates come in all sizes, it is true, from XS to XXXXL, and reportedly engage in ritual circle dances known as Petits Fours, so named because the celebrants Get Down on All Fours.

Sacred to Iota are dots, periods, motes, specks, and other Atoms of Being weighed carefully. She favors those who religiously Cross their Tees, such as initiates of Her Order, the Lesbian Golfers' Association (LGA). These are also given to the rite of Teeing Off, swinging magical wands, called "irons" and "woods," to invoke Her Presence. Many of Her highest observances take place during the summer, when Her priestesses go On Tour.

Iota seems to be invoked frequently as a measure of our emotional caring and commitment when we cry out, "I'll give you not one Iota more!" or "Not one Iota more or less!" Wherefore, many of Her followers claim that She is The True Measure of All Things, and support their observation by pointing out that She stands between Her sisters, ALPHA and OMEGA, well-known extremists. Iota, they say, urges us to Think Small. Skeptics, who say this is only a spotty proposition, remind us of the many invocations to Iota that end with *but,* such as: "Iota love you, *but...,*" "Iota do the laundry, *but...,*" and "Iota be attracted to you, *but....*"

Petty discrepancies aside, it is clear to us that Iota has the stature necessary for a true goddess. So mote it be!

LABOREA is the three-fold, and very busy, goddess of shitwork. As a major Dyke goddess, She shares some ritual observances with CHEMIA, EXERTIA, and even EVACUA. So close is Her relationship with Chemia that OXYDOLY and BONA AMIA are often found within the precincts of shrines to Laborea, small niches in which Her followers keep Her sacred symbol, a Broomstick, which they handle with reverence. These objects must be kept in dark places for it renews their strength. Her observances are shunned by those under the influence of INERTIA.

As the Kitchen Witch, always riding Her sacred Broom, She is the goddess of housework and dear to the Dykes of Domesticity (see Chemia and DOMICILA), often accompanied by her good friends BONA AMIA, PALM OLIVIA, and OXYDOLY. Her image can often be found hanging from a ceiling light or cabinet handle in the kitchens of Her devotees, and Her ritual observances include cooking, washing dishes, doing laundry, and cleaning the toilet (the sacred porcelain* shrines of Evacua). Indeed, Puttering is said to be one of the most sacred rituals for the devotees of Kitchen Witch, and they sometimes wear Her handy symbol attached to one of the belt loops on their jeans, the Whisk Broom. But She does not do windows and is allergic to dust, so you're on your own if you insist on engaging in such rites!

Like FALLOPIA, many of Laborea's rituals are performed only sporadically, when Her worshippers are "in the mood," and, for this reason, She is frequently also associated with spontaneity and those feverish, last-minute rituals before friends are expected to show up for a potluck or party. Her adherents can often be heard muttering an invocation to themselves as they rush around, "Oh shit, I forgot to _____ the _____!," being careful to fill in the blanks.

The origin of this aspect of Laborea is uncertain and ambiguous, as there are so many negative associations with the Kitchen Witch left over from the Burning Days. Some claim that the name dates from the ancient status of wimmin as household slaves, trapped in patriarchal enclaves known as "families," "witch" being used then as a negative term, along with "hag," "crone," and "harpy." Others are swift to point out that the negativity of such words is a man-ipulative ploy of the fathers, used by them because of their fear of the hidden powers of wimmin.

Still others claim that the Kitchen Witch is one of the Good Fairies, or the Little People, who survive into our day in the legend of Sleeping Beauty (an early priestess of Inertia), a story about three witches who undertook to raise a womon-child together. The original womon-centered nature of that story is often overlooked these days because of the many layers of distortion and perverted interpretation introduced by the fathers. But the difficult task of reclamation of our Hera-tage is underway, and the name *Wicca* is once more used to speak of self-empowerment among us. The Kitchen Witch has thus taken up a revered residence in our daily lives again.

As DRUDGEA, Laborea watches over those wimmin who must work in low-paid, exploitative jobs that discourage creativity and dull their aspirations, whether because of their sex, race, physical disabilities, or looks. Drudgea is often invoked on the day sacred to Her, Payday, when it is clear, yet once more, that "ends won't meet," and She is called upon to curse the privileged and wealthy fathers. Other invocations to Drudgea are OHIM (Oh Hell, it's Monday!) and TGIF (Thank goddess it's Friday!), and She smiles upon those who are forced to "put their noses to the grindstone" or labor in "the saltmines." In Her most benevolent aspect, She may even look kindly on the Downwardly Mobile, who seek to divest themselves of unsought privileges, and guide them to a fuller understanding of what privileges are.

Hilaria disrupting the rites of Collatea

As COLLATEA, Laborea's support is sought for the performance of all those unexciting, even unpleasant tasks that seem to be a necessary part of the operation of every wimmin's organization. Particularly sacred to Collatea is the preparation of newsletters and flyers announcing concerts and asking for money, and Her adherents usually gather at least once a month to celebrate Her rituals, circling a table once for each name on a mailing list and performing the sacred tasks of the Stapling, the Folding, the Addressing, and most importantly, the Sorting. Most blessed by Collatea are those who do the Typing and the Mailing, without which there would be no Newsletter in the Mailbox. Because so few are called to these observances, it is also, strangely enough, this aspect of Laborea who promises the most enjoyment, for, as it has been said, wherever three or more Lesbians gather, there will be a party, and So It Is. **HILARIA** has been known to appear most riotously and irreverently at Collatea's rituals, sometimes called "work parties."

Whatever Her aspect, to seek, to know, and to understand Laborea is to grasp infinity. However, it is known that some infinities are more fun than others.

---

*The word *porcelain* is derived from Middle French *porcelaine* 'cowrie shell,' *porcelain*, from Italian *porcellana*, from *porcello* 'vulva,' literally, 'little pig,' from Latin *porcellus*, diminutive of *porcus* 'pig,' vulva; from the shape of the shell—(*Webster's Seventh New Collegiate Dictionary*, p. 661).

LILIHA'ALA'A, * our goddess of Lesbian Sexuality, can frequently be found in the arms of Her Particular Friend, **CUDDLES**, although She associates on a regular basis with a variety of goddesses and often seeks the companionship of **EUPHORIA, HILARIA, EVACUA,** and **EUTOPIA.** So much is She in the Presence of other goddesses that many have trouble knowing for certain when the ritual observances of one have ended and those of another have begun. No one, however, seems to really care, and research on the fine art of hair-splitting on this subject is virtually non-existent, which is just as well.

The rituals of Lilihâalâa are many and diverse. Although some Lesbians have sought to provide initiates with guidelines and manuals detailing Her proper worship, the rituals of Lilihâalâa remain largely an oral tradition, and slips of the tongue often have major (and minor) consequences. The passing on of Her intimate mysteries continues to be regarded as best transmitted as a "hands on" experience that cannot be adequately handled by the conventional methods of books and diagrams.

Lilihâalâa has many aspects familiar to Her devotees: LABIA MAJORA, LABIA MINORA, VAGINA, and CLITORIA (Her hooded aspect— see also **NEMEHA'ALISH**). It is a common practice, when invoking Her, to acknowledge each aspect of Lilihâalâa as the rituals progress by a Laying On of Hands. Worshippers claim that this practice, properly

73

performed, always excites the pleasure of Liliháaláa. Others extol the wonder of Five-Fingered Exercises and Thumbs Up. All agree that each initiate must find her own path to Liliháaláa, and this can take hours.

Because Euphoria is one of Liliháaláa's special companions, their rites often merge and flow one into the other. This process is sometimes called by its esoteric name, "melting." Symbols of Liliháaláa and Her Presence surround us: cowrie shells, orchids, oysters, geodes, irises, canyons, hills, valleys, and certain folds at the base of oak trees. Lip-Service may be paid to Her at any time.

---

*Literally, in Láadan, Liliháaláa means 'wet butterfly,' *lili*, 'to be wet' and *háaláa*, 'butterfly.' See also note at end of **MARIA'** for more information on Láadan.

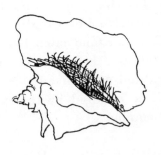

MAGNOLIA, Our Lady of Leisure, is the goddess of Feminist Altruism, and Her devotees claim that there is no higher calling. She abhors those fascinated with survival skills, for She smiles only on those who follow Her path of Self-Sacrifice. These wimmin say it does their hearts good to give of themselves without hope of a Payback or Immediate Return, and they invest much time and energy meeting demands. They shun acting Out of Self Interest, preferring to believe they lack Selfish Motives.

Skeptics, however, who maliciously persist in asserting that no one does anything For Nothing, point to one of Magnolia's sacred observances, the Quest for Altruism Points. This ritual requires at least two celebrants devoted to Feminist Altruism, but more can join in the revels, which have no purpose but the acquisition of points awarded for Acts of Altruism. Any given act can qualify a celebrant for Altruism Points if she can convince the other participants that she was Just Being Nice. She must accomplish this feat by demonstrating that her good deed had absolutely no fringe benefits for her. One Altruism Point is awarded for each Deed enacted "For the Good of All Wimmin." This endeavor is a difficult Task, requiring the stamina for lengthy and unrewarding debate.

This ritual is full of contradictions, as Magnolia's detractors love to point out. If a Deed is, indeed, "For the Good of All Wimmin," and the Seeker must be a womon, then whatever she did **had** to be in her own self-interest. Many seek Altruism Points, but few receive them, for devotees of Magnolia are often seen carrying around lists, called Hidden Agendas, which disqualify them from the ritual. Devotees of Magnolia, however, say that this is one of Her inner mysteries which is too esoteric for skeptics and the uninitiated.

As nearly as we have been able to dis-cover, Magnolia's observances are truly pointless, for we've encountered no one among Her worshippers who has ever received an Altruism Point.

MARIA',* She-of-the-Islands, in the company of Her aspect DOMEDO'OYAA',* is one of the major Found Goddesses of Lesbians everywhere, for Her spheres of influence protect the outcast, the rootless, the wanderers, and the frequent Movers, all those whose homes are the small islands of comfort they make for themselves. Mariá looks fondly upon Movers and Shakers, for they do not stand still. She watches over the oppressed, the disenfranchised, the colonized. Motion, moving, movement are the domain of Mariá. For this reason, whenever the oppressed, the outcasts, band together to fight for their rights, they call their common struggle a "Movement," invoking Mariá's blessing for their efforts.

In Her aspect as Domedóoyaá, The Strong-Hearted-Who-Remembers, Mariá is both the Disperser, or Scatterer, and She-Who-Gathers-Together. As writers like Micheline Grimard-Leduc have said, Lesbians have no country of our own.** If we did once have a native land, say Libya or the Russian steppes, it was taken from us so long ago that we remember it only dimly in our collective dreams, or glimpse its borders when we read *The Wanderground* by Sally Gearhart or *Lesbian Peoples* by Monique Wittig and Sande Zeig. Those scattered by the breath of Mariá can be gathered together by Domedóoyaá once more. So Her devotees say. If the life of each Lesbian is likened to a loose, dangling thread, those threads can be taken up by Domedóoyaá and woven together again in an awesome, magnificent tapestry. By themselves, those single threads

77

Lifting Praises to Mariá

are only what they are. Joined by the artistry of Mariá's vision, they acquire a larger meaning that disrupts the projectors of conventional reality.

So, it is said, the Moving together of Lesbians disturbs the known and the familiar, and what has been will be no more. Our visionaries say that recent earthquakes and eruptions of volcanoes, like that of Mt. St. Helens in 1980, are the passionate tremblings of the Earth, rejoicing that Lesbians are Gathering to dance in our circles again.

Any event that brings Lesbians together celebrates Mariá. It doesn't matter how many attend. Whether it's the Michigan Womyn's Music Festival or an Alix Dobkin concert, a meeting of an incest survivors's group or a rap group on coming out, all is Movement.

One of the most popular and frequent observances of Mariá, which she shares with **DOMICILA,** is called Moving, and Lesbians, who say they will "follow Her anywhere," are much given to frequent enactments of this ritual. When Lesbians celebrate Mariá in this way it is called Moving Day, and almost everyone rises early for the celebration. Those who arrive late for these gala events are required to do penance by chanting hymns, such as "Take Me Home, Country Road" or "Movin' on Up (to the East Side)," while they move the heavy stuff. Many travel light, but others must use trucks, under the auspices of **ASPHALTA,** or invoke one of Her aspects, U-HAUL-IT, said to be an "Adventure in Moving." These Moves often go without a hitch, but Mariá is unpredictable, and the frequent strained muscles and sore backs experienced by those who lift praises to Her are said to be enhancing. Indeed, some maintain that the rites of Moving Day are actually overseen by yet a third goddess, HERNIA. Others contend that Hernia is merely an annoying aspect of Mariá and/or Domicila. In any case, She can be moved by our exertions, and smiles joyously upon us when we bust a gut in Her name.

Followers of Mariá habitually carry sacred volumes, which they call Address Books, and some brag that they have moved as many as six times in one year. These claims are hard to document unless one happens to have been involved in every one of the moves, and Dykes are adept at finding other things to do on Moving Day.

---

*These names, and several others, are created according to the rules of Láadan, a language for wimmin originally constructed by Suzette Haden Elgin.

Literally, in Láadan, *Mariá* means 'one who islands', *mari* = 'island' plus the agentive suffix *á*; *Domedóoyaá* is composed of *dom*, 'remember' and *dooya*, 'strong-hearted,' with the agentive -á attached. *Dooya* means 'Lesbian' in Láadan.

For more information on Láadan, see Suzette Haden Elgin, *A First Dictionary and Grammar of Láadan*, (Madison, WI: SF3, 1985). Available from SF 3, Box 1624, Madison, WI 53701-1624 for $8.00 plus $1.50 for postage. There's also a read-along tape that goes with the grammar/dictionary, available from Suzette Haden Elgin, Route 4, Box 192-E, Huntsville, AR 72740, for $3.00, postpaid.

A second edition, with an English-Láadan dictionary, is now available. Contact SF 3 at the address given above for publication date and price.

**Micheline Grimard-LeDuc, "The Mind-Drifting Islands" in *Trivia* 8 (Winter 1986, p. 28-36).

MOOLA-MOOLA, perhaps the most sought-after and elusive goddess, attracts both the simple and compounded interest of Dykes. She is said to abide in Financial Security, and Her sacred tokens, small disks cut from different metals and rectangular pieces of green paper with mysterious numbers, like 1 or 5 or 10, printed on them, are often carried in the pockets of Her devotees, who believe that bearing these tokens close to their bodies may cause them to multiply. (There are stories told of some who claim to have seen Her tokens with numbers of 50 and 100 on them, but such tales are hard to verify.) Initiates have been known to call these tokens "Bread" for their life-sustaining qualities.

Two of Her better-known aspects are CASHIA and VISA; hardly anyone has heard of CARTA BLANCHA in these latter days, for She is now a "lost goddess." However Moola-Moola is worshipped, Her sensitive priestesses are known as Legal Tenders and they are good at counting. Some, called Tellers, are known for their psychic powers, and their wisdom is likened to that of the Delphic Oracle. They give no Credit to men.

Moola-Moola's minor temples are found on virtually every corner, and one may seek Her bounty at these Automatic Teller Machines 24 hours a day (or night). These shrines, placed conveniently for personal acts of devotion, will dispense Her gifts only if one has what is called a Balance. Sincerity is not enough for seeking Moola-Moola. For this reason, on Payday (when we celebrate the rewards of DRUDGEA—see **LABOREA**), the devout can be seen rushing to one of Her shrines to engage in the ritual of Depositing the Paycheck, said to avert Her dread-ful wrath and being punished by receiving notice of Bouncing Checks, nasty little demons that cost $10 every time they appear. Moola-Moola's displeasure is frequently announced by one of Her malevolent aspects, TELECHECK.

One of Moola-Moola's most common and familiar rituals is that of Balancing the Checkbook, said to ward off Bouncing Checks (but not always effective) when faithfully observed at least once during a lunar cycle. Some believe this ritual enactment is related to, and derived from, ancient rites and rituals concerned with the Balance of Nature, She-Who-Cannot-Be-Fooled. This alleged connection is tenuous, however, because our modern ritual is so rarely marked by the joyous atmosphere it is said attended the older observances. Balancing the Checkbook, while an official observance of Moola-Moola, is often disrupted by a notice from one of Her demon aspects, known in some areas as CHECKRITE. Too frequent periods of Withdrawal, however spiritual in intent, have been known to result in a state of depletion known as being Overdrawn.

Others claim to have dis-covered an ancient relationship between Moola-Moola and **FALLOPIA**, since Balancing the Checkbook must be observed once a month, the period sacred to Fallopia, and requires a facility with Numbers and Counting, both well-known domains of Fallopia's influence. While this connection is certainly plausible, some initiates discount it as counterfeit, and warn of the dangers of Hera-sies like Passing the Buck and Penny-pinching. Similar purported intertwinings of Moola-Moola and other goddesses are many and not to be counted on.

Other rituals dedicated to Moola-Moola seek Her generous bounty or offer thanks for gifts already bestowed. These often involve burning candles or incense in Her sacred color, green, and reciting well-known invocations. Moola-Moola is so diverse in Her aspects, Her influence so pervasive in our daily lives, that Her followers have created many ways of calling upon Her Presence. Those seeking only a moderate gift, for example, or aspiring to peek into the realm of Upward Mobility, may burn a small green candle and chant:

> Moola-Moola, it's no joke,
> I don't like being broke.

Or, those devoted to wallowing in the generosity of Moola-Moola may use a stronger charm:

> Moola-Moola, be a honey,
> Kindly send me lots of money.

Much depends upon the seeker having a positive attitude, so adding adverbs like *kindly* to one's invocations, while no guarantee of the desired response from Moola-Moola, will at least insure Her attentive ear. More importantly, should Moola-Moola smile upon one of us, we cannot forget appropriate thanks for Her giving, and the following song sounds tinklingly to Her, especially if accompanied by shaking Susan B. Anthony dollars together in both hands. The more, the better.

> Moola-Moola, thanks a million,
> Next time, please, make it a billion!

Don't forget to say "please" or Her Legal Tenders may discover they made an Error in Your Favor and take it back!

In some places, like Illinois and New York, Moola-Moola is worshipped as MOOLAH-MOOLAH (a patriarchal corruption of Her Name!), or in various aspects like LOTTA, LOTTERIA, and INSTANT MONEY. These rituals require offerings of specific quantities of Her tokens at designated shrines, for which the devotees receive small cards with hidden numbers on them. In an act known as "Scratching the Surface," the worshipper dis-covers the numbers printed on her cards, thereby determining if Her invocations to Moola-Moola have earned Her blessing. It is said that using one of Moola-Moola's silver tokens, now rare, is an especially good way to rub Her the right way. Other aspirants, claiming that such rituals leave much to chance, regard them as suspect, preferring to acknowledge Moola-Moola by "The Wearing of the Green."

With all due credit to the economy, the worship of Moola-Moola has earned increasing interest in recent years. Many Lesbians, however, feeling that Her praises have been inflated and over-rated, sensing that many of Moola-Moola's institutions have become Bankrupt, are turning to the worship of other goddesses, such as ALTERNATA ECONOMIA, sometimes invoked as BAR TER. Or, shunning such things as Gross and Net Profit, others are calling upon COMMUNITAS or AGRARIA for their most basic needs. They tend, it is said, to coining phrases and mint teas.

All of Moola-Moola's aspects should be checked out.

MUNCHIES, Our Goddess of Easy Eating, delights in fast feasting and junk foods. Her observances are sometimes called Quick Services. Her devotees can sometimes be seen running into one of Her shrines with the Golden Arches at strange hours of the night. Others, perhaps also lolling in the Presence of **INERTIA**, have been heard solemnly intoning, "You can't eat just one." These latter are so wary of unnecessary motion that they are prone to the ritual of "eating in," invoking Munchies' Presence by dialing Her seven sacred numbers. Criticized for what some say is gross indulgence, they point with much pride to the speed with which they can summon Munchies, especially Her aspect known to the faithful as DOMINA's PIZZA.

Because of Munchies' diverse aspects, Her worship is fast-spreading, and this increase in Her popularity has been linked by some to the development of **ASPHALTA's** car cult. Indeed, even their primary symbols show remarkable similarities: Asphalta's intersecting webs, Munchies' chains. Additional evidence for an intimate relationship between these two goddesses can be adduced from the fact that many of Munchies' sacred shrines lie along the pathways traveled by Asphalta's devotees. On the other hand, it may be that the priestesses of Munchies are taking advantage of the convenience afforded by Asphalta's highways and byways. Whatever the nature of the relationship, the golden arches of Munchies' shrines continue to appear beside the lanes of INTERSTATIA, and offer solace to many a weary Journeyer. One of Her most familiar aspects, QWIK-STOP, frequently brags that "There's one in your neighborhood!" Munchies is *never* far from us, and in our greatest need, She makes Instant Gratification easy. Her followers rarely stand in line.

Recent research has suggested another relationship between Munchies and **CHEMIA**, for it has been observed that Munchies appears shortly after one of Chemia's rituals. It is true that devotees of Chemia often invoke Munchies within moments of partaking of one of Chemia's esoteric substances. This, they say, results from the oneness of mind and body. Because the rites of Chemia may lead to those of Munchies, those seeking heights of ecstasy keep relics sacred to Munchies "on hand," and, under the auspices of the Kitchen Witch, will bring out rich delicacies such as the Chips of Potata, Califia's Dip, and gummy bears of many flavors. During High Observances, one may expect to find items sacred to **CHOCOLATA**, Her "Kisses" and M & Ms.

Munchies is called by many names in many tongues: Sara Lee, Submarina, Hamburga, Frita, Wendy, The Dairy Queen, and Lady of the White Castle (both believed by some to have survived into our age from our most ancient sources), Lesbo Zesto, Pizzaria, The Whole Enchilata, and Jill-in-the-Box, one of Her prankster aspects. Recently, we've been told, a patriarchal group calling themselves "Monterrey Jacks" tried to fool the faithful, but every shrine to Jill-in-the Box has been re-covered. In addition, She has countless minor aspects, such as 'Greasy Spoon,' and 'Eats,' and these shrines are announced by flashing neon signs that can be seen for miles.

Her holy places include drive-through windows, from which Her priestesses dispense Her favors (for a donation, of course), and pilgrims seek sustenance at Her temples at their convenience. Consequently, such shrines are called "round the clock" or "24-hour stores." Munchies' sacred numbers murmured with awe and reverence, are 7 and 11.

Initiates into the holy mysteries of Munchies are required to memorize the entire Baskin Robbins' flavor list. After successful completion of this arduous test of their faith, they are then given a list of items at 3:00 A. M. one long night in the deep of winter (usually around February 2, a traditional initiation festival). The priestess, chanting "Aren't you hungry now?," gives them their sacred charge, to find all the items on the list and return with them within the hour. These lists often contain the names of Munchies' most esoteric relics, such as bean burritos, sopapillas, individual anchovy pizzas, pints of Breyer's Blackberry Swirl or Haagen Dasz's Chocolate Chocolate Chip Ice Cream. Because of their difficulty, these initiations recall ancient tests of worthiness, like the Quest for the Grail. Failure to bring back even a single item can result in the candidate's disqualification, and she must then wait yet another year for entrance into the profound Mysteries of Munchies. In this event, she may also be forbidden to worship at even minor shrines and temples, like Ms. Donuts or Long Jane Silver's.

Munchies' rituals are opened by a priestess, who solemnly chants, "Two all-beef patties special sauce lettuce cheese pickles onions on a sesame seed bun." Should she succumb to the wiles of **ANOMIA** and falter on even one syllable, she must begin the chant again. Many of Munchies' devotees maintain that Her Mysteries date back to earliest antiquity, and they cite as evidence one of Her most visible aspects, McDonald, whose name, they believe, is derived from the ancient Celtic goddesses, Macha and Danu.

Cluster forming around a priestess of Nebula

NEBULA, the Shining One, The Radiant One, is the goddess of the Lesbian Star System. The devout frequently worship Her in shrines called book and record stores, where they buy Nebula's artifacts for private enjoyment. She is also worshipped in confluences, large and small, variously referred to as "concerts," "festivals," or "readings," where the ritual performances of Her priestesses, called Stars (or Movement Heavies if loved by **ROTUNDA**) can be observed. Those who religiously attend the rites of Nebula are said to be Fans, but the origins of this title remain nebulous. Some re-searchers, after poring through great clusters of Spiral notebooks, speculate that these followers are called Fans because of the air currents generated by the custom of striking their hands together. Others maintain that the title reflects their tendency to travel widely in circles. Much is hazy.

While Nebula's rituals occur at all times of the year, and in nearly every city with a large Lesbian population, She is best known for the ecstatic reveling which occurs at Her major observances, known as Summer Festivals. These Festivals, often attended by several thousands of Nebula's most devoted fans, are truly the major celebrations of Lesbian culture, for **ELECTRA, EUTOPIA/DYSTOPIA**, and many other goddesses share these performances. The Enlightened call their rituals Star Worship, and many pierce their ears and wear one or several star-shaped earrings as symbols of their loyalty. Others call these Star-Trippers for their habit of traveling great distances to gaze upon one of Nebula's priestesses.

Where one of Nebula's Chosen will appear, large clouds gather. Attendance, measured by a device called a Sliding Scale, is much counted on, and Receipts, offerings at The Door, signify a Star's popularity. Skeptics observe that the more Stars who perform at Nebula's spectacles, the more Fans who attend. Small bands of Leaping Lesbians, said to be quarky, are so transported by these celebrations that they dwell eternally in the Zone of the Free Radicals.

Invocations to Nebula are numberless, but the devout have pinpointed some of great antiquity that never fail to work. If one wishes to address Her, she must begin her correspondence by chanting:

> Glitter, glamour, Nebula,
> Now I wonder where you are.

Should a follower seek a Star's Special Favor, excessive flattery is said to work every time, particularly for Shooting Stars, which glimmer quickly on their way.

> First Spark, Fine Spark,
> One Star I spy tonight.
> Here a quark, there a quark,
> Shine for me your light tonight.

(Speed is of the essence with this incantation.)

The name Nebula has been a source of conjecture in recent days. Some thearists maintain that Her name derives from the constellation of Stars who embody Her presence in this world. Others, perhaps less dazzled by Her charisma and stage presence, insist that Her name actually refers to the constellation of lights that shine upon Her priestesses as they preside at rituals.

Some of Nebula's priestesses are the best-known of all the modern-day priestesses, and indeed, appear to have their own cults, complete with multitudinous "fans" (which contribute to the opinion that these priestesses are "very cool"), and many cult objects, books and recordings, that preserve their words and music for all to enjoy. These, it is said, outshine all others, for they demand astronomical fees, and have great influence. Clusters of nonbelievers scoff at Star Worship, calling it gasly and just so much hot air, but ardent Fans claim that the Stars beloved of Nebula, especially those who are Outfront Lesbians, make all Lesbians visible, forming recognizable patterns that connect us all. Without these Stars, they believe, none of us would Shine.

This debate cannot be taken lightly.

NEMEHA'ALISH,* the hooded aspect of LILI-HA'ALA'A is much-sought after among the devout, but Hers is a temperamental nature, and She is known as much for Her inexplicable indifference as She is for Her equally mysterious passionate outbursts. She is our goddess of physical pleasure, sexual desire, and pure lust. One or more, depending on taste and opportunity, may give tongue to the invocations that excite Her interest and call Her forth.

Her rituals are practiced within the tender wings of Liliháaláa, LABIA MAJORA and LABIA MINORA. During Her most intense rituals, She is known for her multiple, ecstatic appearances, which are accompanied by profuse outpourings of energy and fervor. When Her devotees sense Her imminent arousal, they frequently rise to the occasion with much noise, thrashing about, and loud moans, all of which are said to whet Her appetite and heighten the ecstatic experience of Her arrival. Motion, e-motion, and com-motion attend Her.

When She isn't interested, however, no amount of coaxing or teasing will call Her forth from the folds of Her indifference. For this reason, She is greatly respected, and much care is taken to insure that the proper mood and setting are chosen for Her rituals. Some celebrants take much time preparing themselves and their surroundings to invoke Her, lighting many colored candles, burning incense, smearing their bodies with perfumes, oils, whipped cream, or the essence of **CHOCOLATA**. Others, knowing Her unpredictability well, delight Her with spontaneity and the impulse of a moment. Her worship is usually conducted by hand and mouth, but there is also an occasional Rub, which no one seems to mind as long as it's not the wrong way. When the mood is right, Nemeháalish responds. She cannot be understood, only experienced.

Her gifts, as well as Her mysteries, are legend among the loose of tongue. Only one sincere devotee is necessary to invoke Her Presence, so She is also the goddess of self-love and masturbation. One or more who call upon Her are occasionally assisted in their observances by VIBRATA, She Who Hums Steadily.

Worshippers of Nemeháalish know many times and ways of calling upon Her, and many stories are told of the strange and different places where they have experienced Her ecstasies. It is said they take much delight in vying with one another as they share their tales of risk and daring, in bathtubs, moving vehicles, stopped elevators, sleeping bags under the stars, and in the Earth's many lakes and oceans. Some say that it is possible, but unlikely, that these stories have been exaggerated. It is true that one has to be There.

Whatever one's pleasure, Nemeháalish's rituals remain primarily private, hands-on affairs. Where Her attention is desired, She can be touched by murmuring the chant,

> Nemeháalish, moist with gentle rubbin',
> Peek to me, sweet pleasure's nubbin.

She appears.

*Nemeháalish is composed of the Láadan word for 'pearl', *nem*, with the degree marker *-háalish*, which means 'to an extraordinary degree', attached. Because consonants cannot occur in clusters, Láadan requires an 'e' to be inserted between consonants occurring together as a result of compounding or other morphological processes. This 'e,' however, is not pronounced.

Some of the rituals of Chocolata and Liliháaláa are virtually indistinguishable.

PARANOIA is Our Goddess of the Ever-Watchful. Her eyes are always upon us, even in the Heart of Texas, and She watches over all Lesbians, who know Paranoia in all Her aspects. Especially dear to Her, though, are those who have chosen the treacherous path of Political Activism, those who flaunt their Lesbianism (however casually), and those who live "out front" (rather than "out back") as Lesbians. When a Lesbian walks forward with her head turned to look in back of her, or, at the mention of spray-painting or vandalism, whispers urgently into her telephone, "My line is tapped," then she is said to "be Paranoid," imbued with the spirit of Paranoia. Her devotees regard this as a sign of en-lightenment, and will often vie with one another in their demonstrations of mistrust and suspicion. Truly, it is said, "If I'm Paranoid, "they" must be after me."

Paranoia dogs the footsteps of every outfront Lesbian, lurks deep in the recesses of walk-in closets, and peers furtively around the lentil and cheese potluck casserole. For this reason, and no other, Her Presence can be invoked at any moment, in any place, whether She's needed or not. She is with us when we walk down the street arm-in-arm, when we kiss in public places, especially airports and restaurants, or write "Lesbian Money" on the tokens sacred to **MOOLA-MOOLA**. She is with us when we make love on beaches or in meadows, when we scrawl "Lesbians Ignite" in the shrines sacred to **EVACUA** with our purple magic-markers, and in our cars with bumper stickers that declare, for all the world, "You Bet We're Good Friends" and "The Goddess Is Coming, and Is She Pissed!" Because She is always There, She is always Here, and this is one of Her great Mysteries. It is understood without being understood.

Always, Paranoia assures us, THEY are after us, and these demons have many aspects and guises to fool even the most Paranoid among us. Some demons have cryptic names, like USPO, FBI, CIA, and IRS. Others can be friends, cohorts, or parents, and THEY are much given to listening in on phone conversations, opening your mail, whether you've read it or not, and overhearing whispered confidences in delicatessens. Devotees touched with Paranoia know that "the walls have ears," "money talks," and "the eyes have it." The world is overrun with such wonders.

Paranoia speaks to us when we least expect it, and it is Her Voice we hear in the crackles, bleeps, and buzzes that interrupt our conversations, warning us that our phones are tapped. We can invoke Her by uttering any of Her sacred words, singly or in combination, "revolution," "overthrow," "blow up," "guerilla tactics." "Molotov Cocktail" is believed to be one of Her most powerful invocations, for demons swarm when it is intoned with the sincerity of the devout.

It is the spirit of Paranoia causing the Juice of Adrenalin to flow in our veins when we experience Verbal Harassment in the streets. Jeers, shouts, and insults from men instantly alert Paranoia to our plight, for She knows that what they call "friendly" and "hostile" are one and the same. When you walk the streets and are assaulted by shouts of "Hey Fatty," "Talk to me Cutie," or "Wanna fuck?," remember that Paranoia is at your side through fight or flight. Knowing one of **GETTUFFA**'s Martial Arts will greatly improve your confidence, and sturdy shoes blessed by **PEDESTRIA** help, too.

The suspicious glance of Paranoia can reveal to us the tell-tale signs that a letter or package has been opened by the U. S. MALES, and one of Her most protective rituals is performed periodically by the Ambitious Amazons, the Act of Heavy Stapling. This ritual is so effective, the frustrated say, that the Ambitious Amazons are the only Lesbians who can staple a newsletter so thoroughly that the next issue of *Lesbian Connection* will be out before you can open the current one.

For all these reasons, and more (which we cannot disclose here), Paranoia is The-Goddess-of-Many-Variables. Sacred to Her is the observance "Taking Care of Business." In the truest sense, it is She who helps us to maintain our clarity and vision, enabling us to laugh at the Dirty Joke, Patriarchy, as Mary Daly the Haggard* has observed. Dwellings where Paranoia reigns are easily identified by windows covered by thick curtains or black paint, and the doors may have three or more locks of different types. Especially sacred to Paranoia is the Dead Bolt, which is said to ward off the prying imps and demons of the FBI, CIA, and NARCs. Keeping Paranoia in our minds and hearts, walking with Her Presence before *and* behind us, we may not be safe, but we're harder to nab.

---

*See Mary Daly's distinction between "titters" and "the roaring laughter of women" who see through the Dirty Joke in *Gyn/Ecology* (Boston: Beacon Press, 1978), p. 17.

PEDESTRIA cares for the footsore; She is the Preserver of Soles and the Protector of Heelers. Feet are sacred to Her, so anything involving the feet or use of the feet is right up Her alley. Foot travelers and hitchhikers call frequently upon Her on the road, and sensible footwear is one of Her sacred attributes. It is said, "A good shoe on the foot is worth two in the mouth." To be called a "Goody Two Shoes" is insulting, but we're not sure why. Why should Two Good Shoes be less worthy than One? Scholars of Pedestria's mysteries hold their tongues when asked, and walk quickly away.

Choice of appropriate footwear for all occasions is governed by Pedestria, and Her initiates call frequently upon Her various aspects for guidance when attiring themselves: NIKE, CONVERSA, PUMA, J. C. PENNEY, FAMOLARE, BIRKENSTOCKIA, and PAYLESSA. Pedestria Herself protects jaywalkers, and Her true believers never hesitate to cross against the light. Indeed, they regard it as a serious offense to Her to heed a "Don't Walk" sign, and they are likewise prone to ignore "Don't walk on the grass" signs because they deny the essence of Her Be-ing. Her priestesses are said to be "The Street Wise."

New shoes should always be blessed by Pedestria before serious wearing, but after the "breaking in" period, in a ritual which dedicates them to Her protection. All participants must enter the circle barefooted, as they entered the world, for this signifies their need to be Shoed. The circle is cast and Pedestria is invoked. The celebrants sit in a circle for the Purification of the Feet. Each womon first dips her left foot into a bowl of herb water (Pedestrian herbs such as sage or rosemary are especially recommended), then puts that foot in the lap of the womon seated to her left, who massages the foot with sea salt. After the left foot has been massaged, the womon rinses it in the herb water again, and the womon on her left gently rubs the foot with oil or lotion. When these loving attentions have been lavished on the *left* foot, the same procedure is followed for purifying the right foot of each womon. It is important to begin with the left foot, rather than the right one, for Pedestria is a sinister goddess, and She delights in rituals like Take Back the Night Marches.

When both feet of each celebrant in the circle have been rinsed and well-massaged, everyone puts on her new shoes and places a candle, matching her shoes, into the center of the circle. Each womon should then pass each foot slowly over the candle flame to bless the shoes, invoking the care of Pedestria for each one. If this process is done shoddily, you may find one shoe wearing out faster than the other, discover mysterious holes of unknown origin where some part of the shoe wasn't passed directly over the candle flame, or experience that state of un-Be-ing known as "Down at the Heels." Be sure to ask for protection while traveling on foot. At this point, you can also ask Pedestria to heal your shin splints if you have them, for She is generous and kind to Her followers.

After each womon has invoked the full protection of Pedestria for every eyelet and seam in her shoes, all in the circle join hands and give tongue to any of the countless hymns to Pedestria's praise: "These Boots Were Made for Walking," "Tiptoe Through the Tulips," "I Could Have

Danced All Night," "Walk on By," "Walk a Mile in My Shoes," etc. If you don't know the words, make appropriate noises. Let Pedestria in-spire you and you'll never walk alone. She is never straight-laced. When the merriment has subsided and everything is tied up, open the circle. Pedestria Be.

NOTE: Pedestria considers high-heeled shoes, and any shoes which bind the feet of wimmin, as abominations. Attempts to invoke the blessing of Her for such man-made items of foot apparel always end in embarrassing missteps. Those who usurp Her rituals for shoes with heels more than 1" in height have been known to get their heels caught in sidewalk grates, elevator doors, manhole covers, and catwalks. These are dire feets.

PLACENTA is the goddess of pregnancies, child-birth, miscarriage, abortion, conception, and parthenogen-esis. Where **HILARIA** joins with Her for the Ritual of Par-thenogenetic Inception, there is much cloning about. She begins where the works of **FALLOPIA** end, although some thearists conceive of Her as an aspect of Fallopia because both are goddesses concerned with cycles of wimmin. (Bi-cycles, however, come under the protection of **PEDES-TRIA** and **ASPHALTA**.) Others claim that, because Pla-centa and Fallopia rule the physical processes, that they are both aspects of **EVACUA**. Still others, unplacated by Membrane Only, dismiss any similarities between the two as accidental and could care less.

The thealogical ins and outs of this debate are ovarian in their complexity, and have generated prolonged and over-due debates. While we cannot bear to resolve it here, some evidence for a premature relationship between Fallopia and Placenta is borne out by remembering that the activi-ties of CILIA are said to precurse both of the cycles under the protection of Fallopia and Placenta, respectively. Uri-narily intractable, however, Cilia is rarely observed by the naked eye of womon, and She is known to be fluctuating and wavering in Her e-motions. These are called Fluxes.

Watermelons, parasites, and bloated egos are dear to Pla-centa, and Her observances are often swollen with preg-nant pauses and false starts. Her most sacred ritual is the "Cutting of the Cord," the Rite of Separation, whereby newly-initiated devotees announce their autonomy and responsibility for self-creation. The herbs and potions of **CHEMIA** and INTOXIA which promote clear-headedness are often used in this ritual, and sharp instruments, such as scissors or knives, are offered to Placenta while the initiates chant "I Gotta Be Me."

POLLYANNA (pronounced pól-ya-ná), found often in the company of Her distant cousin **EUTOPIA**, overlooks our fumbling and stumbling, wherefore She is blithely called She-Who-Overlooks. When She reveals Her Self, there is much talk of Visions and Tele-Visions. Her most devoted followers are the Optimistic, for they are said to enjoy a state of perpetual revel-ation. Her priestesses sometimes call themselves Rose-of-This or Rose-of-That, for they habitually wear rose-colored glasses, thereby improving the gift of hindsight.

Pollyanna's shrines, like those of **MUNCHIES**, are found along the byways of **ASPHALTA**, and Her signs say "Scenic Overlook." Worshippers of Pollyanna, overwrought by one of Her Rosy Revel-ations, have been known to skip gaily through the streets crying out, "The revolution's over" and "Lesbianism is no longer an issue." Lesbian skeptics dismiss these proclamations, saying that those who de-light in such optimism are also given to beseeching Pollyanna by mumbling the question, "Why am I surprised?" over and over.

Pollyanna's faithful seem to prefer living in a state of perpetual Surprise, and they will not allow **PARANOIA**'s devotees to observe their rituals. For this reason, information about Pollyanna's sacred gatherings remains mostly hearsay. Diligent re-search has, however, unearthed a few of Her more popular observances, and we will share what we have dis-covered.

One of these rituals begins when Her priestesses gather Her devotees within one of Pollyanna's protected circles. The initiates invoke Her by humming a few bars from "Do You Know Where You're Going To?" while a Rose Bowl, from which everyone sips a nectar called Rosé, is passed carefully around the circle.

The days sacred to Pollyanna are the "good ole days," when there was much talk of Lesbian Nation and The Wanderground, mythical realms of HARMONIA and CON-CORDIA. Those who wish to visit these distant places call upon Pollyanna by chanting,

> Pollyanna, true to Your ways,
> Spirit me back to the Good Ole Days.

This spell is often mis-leading, and some would-be wor-shippers have been known to end up in the 1950s or, alas, as far back as the Burning Time. For which reason, speci-ficity, as usual with goddesses, is far better, and the fol-lowing invocation is more highly thought of:

> Pollyanna, goddess of the found,
> Spirit me to The Wanderground!

Much, however, it is agreed, has been lost.

After their rituals have ended, devotees of Pollyanna are said to nod knowingly at one another, uttering spells, such as "The World's a Rose Garden" or "Life's a Bowl of Cher-ries." Those so in-spired by Pollyanna, knowing neither pits nor falls, prefer their libations unstemmed, striving to be High on Life. One tight-lipped group of Pollyanna's be-lievers claims that "The World is Their Oyster" (Hail Li-liháaláa!), but the dubious disdain Her pearls of wisdom.

PYROMANIA burns passionately for those who choose Her cinder path, and Her flame can be a binding spell. Some claim She is merely incendiary, but a large number have been burned and burned out by Her crimson visage and fiery locks. Without getting caught in the cross-fire of this spiritual debate, we can note here that the burn out typical of Pyromania's most dedicated followers has been confused with similar states among the devotees of **CHEMIA**, **EXERTIA**, and and certain cults associated with **ELECTRA**'s worship.

Her appearances bring not the comfort of a cozy warmth, for She moves always at red heat, like a prairie fire engulfing and devouring whatever's in Her path, including Her devotees and their offerings. It is known that the observances of Exertia often lead to the exhaustion sacred to Pyromania, but scholars of the sacred disagree regarding the point at which the worship of Exertia is transformed into the rituals of Pyromania. We have observed good companions, on one day all fired up, on the next all burned out, and we suspect that they have tried the very dangerous ritual called "Burning the Candle at Both Ends." Only the most adept have survived this consuming ritual. So close are the ritual observances of Pyromania and Exertia that some devotees of **DEA ABLEA**, performing a ritual known as "Burning Calories," have unwittingly strayed into Pyromania's path and fallen there. This we have on good authority.

One scholar, burning the midnight oil, has dis-covered what she believes to be a little-known connection between our current rash of burn out victims and our losses during The Burning Time. She points out that the patriarchs have become more clever at devising methods to extinguish us. During The Burning Time, they were satisfied with destroying our bodies. Now, they ignite our spirits with dreams of freedom and justice, and, afire with righteous anger, we gladly throw ourselves into this cause and that movement. Enflamed, crying out, "Light my fire!," we rush hither and thither until Pyromania consumes our flickering and sputtering energies.

The feverish activities of Pyromania's devotees call to mind the whirling dervishes of the Spin Cycle sacred to Electra, to whom Her observances are often likened. While we acknowledge the similarities that might lead one to confuse Pyromania with Electra, their outward signs appearing to be almost identical, we believe the tendency to confuse their worship is due entirely to the fact that Exertia's strenuous rituals are related to those of Pyromania, Electra, and **LABOREA** as well. We suggest that, following our most reliable sources, there are many Ways to achieve the state known as "being fried."

Pyromania's sacred color is gold, and Her presence can be invoked by setting fire to any flammable object. The green paper tokens sacred to **MOOLA-MOOLA** are especially good because they burn easily and quickly, particularly when in Pockets. Hence the practice, popular among Pyromania's followers, called "Burning Money." Her Presence, for those who care, can be invoked by the query, "Where's the fire?" Pyromania abhors offerings like candles and other limited fires, for She thrives only on blazes Out of Control. Moisture and dampness of any kind are anathema to Pyromania, and Her unwanted attentions can be discouraged by throwing cold water on them. Truly, it is said, "Where there's smoke, there's Pyromania," and many a Lesbian has felt Her heated breath.

106

QUIETUS is the demon of male-identification, and his symbol is the forked tongue of doublespeak, the Y, which sign is sacred to those who say not what they mean and mean not what they say, the Schools of Snools.* He is often found skulking around the celebrations and revelations of Lesbian gatherings. He feeds voraciously on vibrant gynergy and has shown himself adept at hitching rides on in-spiration.

Although many Lesbians have sworn to eliminate Quietus, he's difficult to identify for he can make himself invisible at will. In his worst deceit, he can take on the appearance of the Haggard and cause those he infiltrates to seem to speak with utter wisdom, insight, and clarity. For this reason, Quietus is a bothersome parasite, and he is certain to appear wherever there is oppression, repression, and depression.

The symptoms associated with possession by this demon include withdrawal from revel-ation, a morbid desire for "perfection," a refusal to talk about any subject except the "right" and the "wrong" of it—from the relative "purity" of marbled halvah to the inherent "naturalness" of eating with one's fingers—loss of the desire to dance, skip, and sing, and vague feelings of dis-quiet that cannot be named. Wimmin who sense his presence may sigh deeply and say, "She really put a quietus on everything." Failing to perceive that the demon of male-identification is responsible for another woman's behavior, we blame her, instead, thereby pleasing Quietus greatly. He in-spires those who indulge in his observances, called Blaming the Victim and Horizontal Hostility.

Quietus' favorite mode of moving himself from one community to another is called the Vicious Cycle, for he furiously pedals resentment, recrimination, rejection, and revenge. Once the Vicious Cycle of Blame, Defense, Charge, and Counter-Charge is set in motion, the only sure way of braking it is to identify the presence of Quietus, and quickly offer support to the wimmin he has spooked.**

Exorcisms to rid a womon of this demon are lengthy and tedious, but so is the snarl of his snooling. Solace during periods of Quietus may be sought by invoking various goddesses, such as **EUPHORIA**, **ELECTRA**, **EVACUA**, **CUDDLES**, and **EUTOPIA**. Their Presences, one or several, are frequently soothing and uplifting during painful transits, giving us assurance that we can, indeed, "get through this," too. But it is **HILARIA**, and Her companions, CHUCKLES, CHORTLES, GIGGLES and GUFFAWS, who excel in dis-spelling Quietus. Because he thrives on missed-communication and mixed messages, Quietus cannot survive Be-Laughing***, the lusty e-ruptions of uncontrolled revel-ation. Where Lesbians are gladly and habitually Out of Order, Quietus cannot remain for long!

---

*A *snool* is "a cringing person. ...sadism and masochism combined, the stereotypic saints and heroes of the sado-state," Mary Daly, *Pure Lust*, (Boston: Beacon Press, 1984), p. 20-21.
**On spooking, see Mary Daly and Jane Caputi, *The Wickedary*, p. 229.
***See note at the end of Hilaria.

ROTUNDA, the Folded One, is widely worshipped, especially by Her Chosen, the Fat Dykes, who follow Her round-about paths and circumlocutions. She is a kind and generous goddess, lavishly bestowing Herself amid the rolls and folds of Her devotees. On those She enfolds, Her blessings are called "Love Handles," for their esoteric uses in the rituals sacred to **LILIHA'ALA'A**. Her priestesses are reputed to be among the most well-rounded Dykes found anywhere, and they are called Zaftig.

Some authorities say there is mounting evidence of Lesbians hostile to Rotunda's magnificence, and they cite rumors of clandestine meetings, called Cambridge Diets, where Lesbians starve themselves for affection. Others mention Dykes possessed by ANOREXIA and BULIMIA wasting themselves in cruel practices that leave them fat-free. Indeed, we have heard stories of Lesbians so fearful of Rotunda that they are ever pursued by the demons of Weight Watchers, who are much given to the vile ritual of Counting Calories, for they aspire to weightlessness.

Rotunda heartily approves of full-bodied invocations, and finds most appetizing any who approach Her with guttural rumblings and largesse. As the number of Her devotees continues to expand, so, too, do the invocations known to appeal to Her taste. Rotunda's generous proportions can be sought by the following invocation, sometimes called the Fat Blessing. It is known to carry weight with Her:

Rotunda the Large, Rotunda the Great,
Enfold my body, for I love my weight.

Terms like "roly-poly," "chubby," or "obese" displease Her, and must be avoided by those who seek Her.

Rotunda, it should be noted, abhors the sickly aftertaste of Diet Sodas, for these are consumed in great quantities by the followers of the false goddesses, Jane Fonda and Crystal Light. No one dares step light 'n' lively at Her observances, for She attends only to the weighty tread of the elegantly fat, and cherishes their bouncing breasts and generous flesh.

A devotee of Inertia experiencing the wrath of the triple Goddess Tofu—Miso—Soya

TOFU, MISO, and SOYA name the triple goddess of natural foods, She-Who-Decides-What-Is-Good-For-You. They are most often represented sitting together atop a compost heap or midden, with wreaths of wheat grass, oats, and alfalfa sprouts upon their bran-colored brows. Their believers eschew all red meats, refined sugars, and white flour, and are said to engage in orgiastic rituals during which they ingest huge quantities of garlic cloves, said to be an aphrodisiac, and brewster's yeast. Some adepts are said to be so transported by these observances that they enter into the transcendent state of Fermentation where they bubble with much spirit. While the esoteric significance of these rituals remains obscure, some experts believe that these activities are a type of sympathetic magic used to aid the rising of seven-grain bread dough.

The most sacred ritual dedicated to the worship of Tofu, Miso, and Soya is the Rite of Recycling, not to be confused with the rituals sacred to **FALLOPIA** or **PEDESTRIA**. The fastidious practitioners of this rite divide their garbage with great care into Organic and Nonorganic. Organic Garbage, so called for its readily identifiable odor, includes eggshells, coffee grounds, thrice-used tea leaves, corn husks, tomato ends, and the well-browned leaves of lettuce. These offerings are added to sacred Compost Heaps at least once a week, and then carefully worked in with previous offerings. This process is said to produce much heat as Bacteria and Earthworms, the Little Folk much-beloved of Tofu, Miso, and Soya, consume the offerings,

111

thereby Recycling them. A "rich" Compost Heap is believed to be a sign of great virtue.

Nonorganic Garbage is faithfully divided into various types: the Aluminum, the Metal, the Glass, the Newspapers. Each type of Nonorganic Garbage to be Recycled is allotted its own sacred Garbage Can, and woe unto her who is ignorant enough to put Glass into the Aluminum container, or Aluminum into that reserved for Metal. These are grave errors for they expose a lack of proper concern for the worship of Tofu, Miso, and Soya. The particularly devout are rumored to sort the Glass containers into Brown, Green, and Clear, but our re-searches have failed to turn up grounds for this. The less fanatical occasionally offer up used brown bags and glass jars to Her priestesses at the temples of Tofu, Miso, and Soya—called Food Coops— where the most devoted of Her followers regularly volunteer their labor, thereby earning Members' Discounts. Though the origins of the Ritual of Recycling are uncertain, its rapid spread is evidenced by increasing numbers of Dumpsters and Canisters, shrines, large and small, dedicated to accepting our offerings to Tofu, Miso, and Soya.

Cherished by Tofu, Miso, and Soya are those who plant their own organic gardens and protect the fragile greens from the destructive influences of The Poisonous Pesticides, the DDT, the Dioxin, and others. Her Threefold Protective Blessing can be sought with the following invocation addressed to one of Her minor aspects:

RUTABAGA, Rutabaga, come and bless
My salsify and watercress.

Great faith is also placed in instant invocations, like "Can it!" and "Put a lid on it!," but these are wrapped in mystery. It is said, too, that regular observance of Her rituals will ward off the cancerous presences of the demons BHA, EDP, and the perilous Red Dye #2. Especially sacred to Her Threefold Self is the Mung Bean, and a complicated five-day ritual, called Sprouting, if successful, will earn Her most Bounteous Blessings.

NOTE: There is fuzzy evidence that certain followers of **INERTIA** often feel the displeasure of Tofu, Miso, and Soya when they forget to turn their Left-Overs, sacred to **CHANCY**, into in-spired victuals. Her disapproval is said to reveal itself to these slackards when molds of brilliant hues and bizarre construction appear on Left-Overs. They may or may not announce their appearance with Reek, but, once these growths reside among one's Left-Overs, the Threefold Threat of Tofu, Miso, and Soya's displeasure can only be averted by immediately making an offering of them to a Dumpster, Canister, or Compost Heap. Truly, it is said, "We have nothing to lose."

TRANSPORTIA, in Her mundane aspect, is the goddess of all those who travel the round-about paths of public transportation to their destination, and Her devotees are called variously, Riders, Commuters, or Subway Rats (whence the phenomenon known as "The Rat Race," one of Her sacred observances). So circuitous and convoluted are Her Routes that they are said to be A-mazing and are frequently likened to the webbery of Ariadne, a lost goddess. She watches over the journeys of all who use busses, taxis, airplanes, trains, and subways, and Her Presence is often invoked by those rushing to any of Her shrines or temples. The shrines dedicated to Her observances are marked by little square signs, usually above the horizon, that say "Bus Stop," "Subway," or large green signs, often on INTERSTATIA, with the sacred symbols "Airport" or "All Trains," for Her major temples.

The appropriate way to invoke Transportia's blessing for the Rushing Ritual is to chant, while running and panting,

Good Transportia, I make this rhyme:

Get me to the $\begin{Bmatrix} \text{bus} \\ \text{train} \\ \text{plane,} \\ \text{etc.} \end{Bmatrix}$ on time.

All invocations addressed to Transportia require, of course, that the mind of the devotee be on the right track.

She is the special guardian of those called the "Running Late," those who fear that the bus, plane, or taxi will leave them behind or fail to get them "where they want to go" on time. In this circumstance, there is much railing. If you are clearly Running Late, you must acknowledge your responsibility as you invoke Transportia's aid:

> Hail Transportia, hear my plea,
> Make the _____ wait for me.

Fill in the blank with the appropriate aspect of Transportia. Specificity helps.

Also beloved of Transportia are those who practice the mysteries known to initiates as "Making Connections," for, it is said, they are so devoted to the rituals of Rushing and Running Late that they are easily fooled by Transportia's pranks. The ritual of Making Connections is begun when the Commuter or Rider successfully acquires one of Transportia's sacred Tokens, a "Transfer," from the hand of one of Her priestesses, called a Driver or a Conductor, before being trampled underfoot or shoved "to the rear." Its sublime conclusion, the Making of Connections, is only achieved when the individual uses the Transfer within the mysterious Period of Time specified on it, usually within an hour or two and on the "same day of issue." Transportia is a whimsical goddess, of course, and many would-be Makers of Connections have dis-covered, to their grief, that their Transfer is no longer "good" because the priestess gave them one dated for the previous month or marked with a time prior to their act of Embarkation. We have been unable to find out exactly how these priestesses determine the date and time limit for the use of these Tokens, but initiates into Transportia's subterranean mysteries assert that there is, indeed, a system known only to the Transported.

This temperamental goddess is sometimes known as RAP-ID TRANSPORTIA, but those who invoke Her in this way do so only in jest, for She rarely delivers. Like **CHANCY**, She is renowned for Her love of a good joke. And like both **DETOXIA** and DRUDGEA (see **LABOREA**), She can also be difficult and demanding of those who would follow Her routes hoping to reach a Destination. While "on route," the faithful must obey a number of mysterious signs that warn of taboo activities, such as "No Slugs," "No Smoking," "Don't talk to Driver (or Conductor)," "No Spitting," "No Littering,"and "No Loitering." In addition to these numerous taboos, there are cryptic injunctions that must be followed to the letter, such as "Right change only," "Step to the Rear," "Fasten Seatbelts," "All luggage must be under your seat," and "Keep moving forward." Woe unto those would-be followers who try to deceive one of Her priestesses by using a slug instead of one of Her sacred Tokens, or get "on board" without the Right Change, for their Destiny is uncertain!

Various aspects of Transportia are worshipped in different cities: BART (San Francisco), IRT, BMT, and IND (New York), MARTA (Atlanta). Other aspects are more widely reputed, and these include AMA TRAKA, PANNA AMA, and DELTA. It is known that devotees of **DEA ABLEA**, **EXERTIA**, and **TOFU, MISO, and SOYA** are sometimes seen at the shrines of Transportia, but most of these prefer to entrust their modes to the surer auspices of **PE-DESTRIA**, going "on foot."

Those on whom Transportia smiles are said to be "transported," for they have grasped the handy straps that steady and comfort them during the roughest rides. This is one of Her arcane aspects, and only a very few hold onto Her in this meta-physical sense.

UMPIRA/TEMPURA, She-Who-Calls-the-Plays, often stands just behind a Plate where She takes a dim view. Skeptics, who would question Her Calls, allege that an intimate connection between Umpira and Tempura is unlikely, but that can be said of any relationship. In fact, we have it on authority that They have called many diamond celebrations in Their own honor, crowding plates and hearing appeals. In Their dual aspect, They are defensive or offensive, depending on the occasion.

Umpira/Tempura is a rookie in the association of goddesses, having only been dis-covered recently by scouts in the bush leagues, and the dubious say that this cannot be a winning combination. This team works together well, however, for it's Tempura who fires up softball Dykes during really hot games and leaves them fried after too much exertion. Unlike Umpira, Tempura likes batting the ball around and keeps pitchers firing away.

Both are primarily summer goddesses, as heat is properly Their element. For this reason, many of Umpira/Tempura's ritual observances are held during the period that begins soon after the Vernal Equinox and ends with the Autumnal Equinox. Many a pleasant summer night is spent with Her priestesses, called Jocks (for their habit of Jockeying for Position), arranged in a protective figure, The Diamond, while others sit on hard, wooden benches being offensive. The latter take turns swinging a wand, called a Bat, trying to hit the flies so numerous at this time of year. Players who Drop Flies are said to be defensive, and this Act is called an Error. We have, so far, not unearthed a reasonable explanation for this terminology, although scores suggest themselves.

Umpira, true to Her nature, stationed majestically behind the Plate, calls strikes and balls according to Her Blessed Whim. When a Batter has had Three Strikes, Umpira calls her Out, and the disappointed one cannot become a Runner. Instead, she retires to The Bench, where she must sit until summoned once more into the hallowed On Deck Circle. The sacred number Three is pivotal in these rituals, for each group of priestesses is also allotted Three Outs per Inning, and there are Three Sacred Bases which Runners are obliged to touch before they are allowed to approach Home Plate. One of Umpira/Tempura's profound mysteries is called Stealing Bases, and Their devotees are said to Steal Bases whenever they can. Should they fail in an attempt, they are put out.

Umpira/Tempura is also much-beloved of devotees to **PEDESTRIA** and **DEA ABLEA**, and Their priestesses often garb themselves in the habits of Dea Ablea, sweatpants and terry cloth headbands, which soak up the sacred moisture they exude during their rituals. A minor aspect of Umpira, GAMEY (see also **VISCERA**), works part-time officiating Break Ups, for She enjoys keeping Her hand in.

VISCERA is often invoked by those Lesbians who wish to participate in the hallowed rituals of LILI-HA'ALA'A and EUPHORIA with other Lesbians whom they find particularly spiritual. Viscera loves those who follow their Gut Reactions in the ways of Pure Lust. One of Her most familiar aspects is GAMEY, so called for Her elaborate rules and roles, the playing of which are said to de-light Her followers. Gamey's rituals include Dimming the Lights, Playing Soft Music, and Baiting the Hook. Gamey's initiates often invoke Her by whispering, "I'm just a Romantic," as though this incantation were self-explanatory. Skeptics are quick to point out that Gamey's devotees are accident-prone, since they frequently talk excitedly about falling in love, being "in"over their heads, and getting themselves "smitten" time and time again. They are known for their tendency to crushes and smashing, for which reason they must observe Gamey's most esoteric rite, Breaking Up.

Certain priestesses associated with Viscera's worship, calling themselves Relationship Counselors, officiate at these rituals, which can be tedious, drawn out, and extremely painful to the parties involved. The Rite of Breaking Up begins when one partner yells "You done me wrong" at the other, who must then offer the appropriate response, "Breaking up is Hard to do." These sayings and responses fly back and forth until both participants have exhausted their resources. Their relationship is ritually dissolved by a last act of Sharing, eating a bowl of Serial Monogamy.*

Sacred to this aspect of Viscera are red roses, attributes shared by **POLLYANNA** and **CHOCOLATA**, and silly cards that carry an embossed phrase, "For those who care to send the very best." Exact translations of this saying elude us, but those who receive such inscriptions are said to become "mushy."

Many are physically attracted to Viscera, and She is properly worshipped in shrines, called One-Night Stands by Her devotees, which are said to arise spontaneously wherever one or more Lesbians wish to celebrate their sexuality and the pleasures of their senses. Her Presence at a gathering is known by an electric charge, caused by Her magnetic personality, which enlivens the air about us and a tingling, pulsating sensation de-lighting **NEME-HA'ALISH**.

Viscera especially favors those whose fervor prompts them to offer tongue, hand, breast, thigh or buttock for the observances of Liliháaláa, Nemeháalish, or LABIA MAJORA and MINORA in their Quest for Immediate Gratification. Empty matchbook covers with numbers, in groups of seven, written illegibly, are among Her most sacred attributes, Some of Her most ardent followers are said to have large collections of them. Invoking Her by "calling" one of these mysterious numbers is said to be Keeping in Touch or Reaching Out to Someone. These are perilous rituals. Only the most skilled adepts of Viscera should attempt them.

Viscera blesses those who please Her by frequent visitations of spiritual rapture called Love at First Sight.

---

*Thanks to Phyllis Birkby

The YAH-BUT, close cousin demon of QUIETUS, is the repetitive quirky quibbler who doesn't know when to shut up. Yah-But is a dis-ease of the mind known to all Lesbians at one time or another and it's extremely infectious. Once one Lesbian has invoked Yah-But by uttering "Yeah...but" in a discussion, the dis-ease spreads and multiplies itself until everyone is tediously chanting Yah-But, Yah-But, Yah-But.

Yah-But is a deceptive imp, as his name implies. All is implication. What is not, seems to be, or could be, or might be. Yah-But begins by appearing to be positive, affirmative, in agreement. But, then, all is opposition, disagreement, dissimulation, contrary. Yah-But seems to support, then withdraws into a conditional fog. One Lesbian might say, "We could organize a wimmin-only dance," only to hear a chorus of Yah-Buts: "yeah, but what about men," "yeah, but what about male children," "yeah, but what about finding a place," "yeah...but" and so on. Yah-But's sole purpose among Lesbians is to make sure that nothing ever happens.

Yah-But thrives in the state called Stag-Nation,* and will quickly flee at the first sign of activity or movement. The best way to ward off Yah-But seizures is to keep spinning and sparking. So say our healers.

---

*See Mary Daly, *Gyn/Ecology*, p. 6, and *The Wickedary*, p. 229.

WHO TO CALL

CYCLES
Domicila
Nebula
Electra
Pedestria
Fallopia
Placenta
Moola-Moola
Tofu, Miso, and Soya

DWELLINGS
Chemia
Drudgea
Mariá (changes in)
Kitchen Witch
Domicila
Laborea

FOOD
Chancy
Munchies
Chocolata
Tofu, Miso, and Soya

HAPPINESS
Chemia
Dolores
Chocolata
Cuddles
Euphoria
Eutopia/Dystopia
Dea Ablea
Hilaria
Detoxia
Lilih, áaláa
Orgasmia

HEALTH and HEALING
Dea Ablea
Fallopia
Dolores
Inertia/Exertia
Evacua
Rotunda
Tofu, Miso, and Soya

HUMOR CONTROL
Hilaria

INSPIRATION
Chemia
Fallopia
Detoxia
Media
Electra
Nebula
Eutopia/Dystopia

LOVE
Aerea Corrida (long distance)
Lilih+ áaláa
Chocolata
Nemeháalish
Cuddles
Nebula
Digitalis
Umpira/Tempura
Euphoria
Viscera

POLITICS
Anomia
Paranoia
Eutopia/Dystopia
Pollyanna
Magnolia
Pyromania

PROSPERITY
Moola-Moola
Nebula

REALITY CHECKS
Inertia/Exertia
Iota
Pyromania

**SELF DEFENSE/
PROTECTION**
Gettuffa
Paranoia

SILENCES
Anomia
Et Cetera
Errata
Marginalia
Nebula

TRANSITIONS
Domicila
Inertia/Exertia
Evacua
Pyromania

**TRAVEL/
CONNECTIONS**
Aerea Corrida
Nebula
Asphalta
Pedestria
Digitalis
Transportia

Other Titles Available

As The Road Curves by Elizabeth Dean ($8.95) Ramsey had it all; a great job at a prestigious lesbian magazine, and a reputation of never having to sleep alone. Now she takes off on an adventure of a lifetime.

All Out by Judith Alguire ($8.95)
Winning a gold medal at the Olympics is Kay Strachan's all-consuming goal. Kay remains determined, until a budding romance with a policewoman threatens her ability to go all out for the gold.

Lesbian Stages ($9.95) Sarah Dreher's play scripts are treasures: good yarns firmly centered in a Lesbian perspective, peopled with specific, complex, often contadictory—just like real people—characters.— Kate McDermott

Gray Magic by Sarah Dreher (8.95)
A peaceful vacation with Stoner's friend Stell turns frightening when Stell falls ill with a mysterious disease and Stoner finds herself an un-witting combatant in the great struggle between the Hopi Spirits of good and evil.

Stoner McTavish by Sarah Dreher ($7.95)
The original Stoner McTavish mystery introduces psychic Aunt Hermi-one, practical partner Marylou, and Stoner herself, who goes off to the Grand Tetons to rescue dream lover Gwen.

Something Shady by Sarah Dreher ($8.95)
Travel Agent/Detective Stoner McTavish travels to the coast of Maine with her lover Gwen and risks becoming an inmate in a suspicious rest home to rescue a missing nurse.

Morgan Calabresé; The Movie by N. Leigh Dunlap ($5.95)
Wonderfully funny comic strips. Politics, relationships, life's changes, and softball as seen through the eyes of Morgan Calabresé.

Look Under the Hawthorn by Ellen Frye ($7.95)
A stonedyke from the mountains of Vermont, Edie Cafferty sets off to search for her long lost daughter and, on the way, meets Anabelle, an unpredictable jazz pianist looking for her birth mother.

Runway at Eland Springs by ReBecca Béguin ($7.95)
When Anna flying supplies and people into the African bush, finds herself in conflict over her agreement to scout and fly supplies for a game hunter, she turns to Jilu, the woman running a safari camp at Eland Springs, for love and support.

Promise of the Rose Stone by Claudia McKay ($7.95)
Mountain warrior Isa goes to the Federation to confront its rulers for her people. She is banished to the women's compound in the living satellite, Olyeve, where she and her lover, Cleothe, plan an escape.

Order from New Victoria Publishers, P.O. Box 27, Norwich, Vt. 05055